WAR AND PEACE IN TRANSITION

War and Peace in Transition

Changing Roles of External Actors

Edited by
Karin Aggestam & Annika Björkdahl

NORDIC ACADEMIC PRESS

Nordic Academic Press
P.O. Box 1206
SE-221 05 Lund
www.nordicacademicpress.com

© Nordic Academic Press and the authors 2009
Typesetting: Stilbildarna i Mölle, Frederic Täckström
Cover: Jacob Wiberg
Cover images: Mc Namara/Zamur Art/Gamma/IBL; OSCE/Miloslav Rokos;
Kuqi Flaka/Gamma/IBL.
Printed by ScandBook, Falun 2009
ISBN: 978-91-85509-22-5

Contents

About the Authors

Karin Aggestam is Associate Professor in Political Science and Director of Peace and Conflict Research, Lund University. Her research covers areas such as ethics of war and peace, diplomacy, negotiation and conflict resolution, and with a regional specialisation in the Middle East in general and the Israeli-Palestinian conflict in particular. She is presently coordinating a research project on just and durable peace in the Western Balkans and the Middle East, funded by the EU's 7th Framework Programme.

Joakim Berndtsson is a postdoctoral researcher in Peace and Development Research at the School of Global Studies, University of Gothenburg. He recently finished a PhD thesis *The Privatisation of Security and State Control of Force: Changes, Challenges and the Case of Iraq*. He is currently working on a new research project entitled 'Security for Sale: Perceptions of Threat and Security among Private Security Companies', funded by the Swedish Research Council.

Annika Björkdahl is Associate Professor at the Department of Political Science, Lund University. Her research interests concern the influence of ideas and norms in international relations, and the role of international organisations in conflict prevention, management and resolution, particularly in the Western Balkans. She is currently engaged in a research project on Just and Durable Peace by Piece in the Western Balkans and the Middle East funded by the EU's 7th Framework Programme.

Birger Heldt is Director of Research at the Folke Bernadotte Academy, and Associate Professor of Peace and Conflict Research. He has been project leader at the Swedish National Defence College, and post-doctoral fellow at Uppsala University and Yale University. His current research is mainly concerned with peacekeeping operations and preventive diplomacy.

Kristine Höglund is Associate Professor at the Department of Peace and Conflict Research, Uppsala University. Her research covers issues such as the dilemmas of democratization in countries emerging from violent conflict, the importance of trust in peace negotiation processes, and the role of international actors in dealing with crises in war-torn societies. She recently published the book Peace Negotiations in the Shadow of Violence (2008, Martinus Nijhoff).

Kersti Larsdotter is Research Assistant at the Department of War Studies at the Swedish National Defence College, and a PhD student at the School of Global Studies, University of Gothenburg. Her dissertation concerns military conduct in peace operations and counterinsurgency.

Anna Leander is Professor at the Copenhagen Business School. She works with sociological approaches to international political economy and international relations and has focused on security practices. Her work is published among other places in *Armed Forces and Society, Cooperation and Conflict Journal of International Relations and Development, Journal of Peace Research, The Millennium, Review of International Political Economy* and *Third World Quarterly*. She has recently published *Constructivism in International Relations* (with Stefano Guzzini) and 'Securing Sovereignty by Governing Security through Markets'.

Michael Schulz is Associate Professor in Peace and Development Research, Gothenburg University. His areas of interest are long-term peace-building and intervention in war-torn societies and conflict resolution in Israel/Palestine, Sri Lanka, Iraq, Congo, and Somalia. His most recent publications include 'Reconciliation through education – Experiences from the Israeli-Palestinian Conflict', in *Journal of Peace Education* (2008), 'Hamas Between Sharia Rule and Democracy', in *Peace Building* and *Globalization*, (2007, with Tavares, Rodrigo).

Maria Småberg is Assistant Professor at the Department of History and lectures in Peace and Conflict Research at Lund University. Her dissertation *Ambivalent Friendship. Anglican Conflict Handling and Education for Peace in Jerusalem 1920–1948* (2005) concerns religious and educational peace efforts in Palestine during the British Mandate period. In her ongoing research, she deals with the Swedish missionary Alma Johansson, who witnessed the genocide on the Armenians in eastern Turkey 1915.

Isak Svensson is Associate Professor at the Department of Peace and Conflict Research, Uppsala University. His research has covered issues such as bias and neutrality in international mediation, religious dimensions of armed conflicts, and strategies of third-parties in peace processes. He has published material in *Journal of Conflict Resolution* and *Journal of Peace Research*.

Foreword

I begin by thanking the University of Lund and its Department of Political Science for the superb organisation of the national conference on Peace and Conflict Research held in October 2008. Without such excellent teamwork a book like this would not have been possible.

I am also very pleased to author the foreword of this timely book that deals with the changing roles and practices of external actors before, during and after armed conflict. The issues addressed are related to the challenges that the international community has increasingly faced ever since peacekeeping changed its focus from interstate to intrastate conflicts in the late 1980s. The challenges are not just in terms of meeting capacity needs, but also about how international missions should be carried out. Among the important new challenges are the protection of civilians against atrocities by warring parties, the creation of stable states characterised by good governance, and how to manage spoilers. Important mandated tools to achieve this include an increased permissiveness for peace operations to use armed force, not just in self-defence, but also proactively against actors intending to spoil the peace or committing atrocities against civilians. Other tools are the promotion of security sector reforms and rule of law reforms.

These challenges and tools have in turn not only resulted in increasingly complex and multifunctional peacekeeping operations, but also in the birth of a new type of specialised peace operations that may be called capacity-building missions. The latter type of missions lack an executive mandate, as they focus on building the host states' capacity in areas such as rule of law, good governance, human rights and democratic control of the security sector. Multifunctional, complex peace operations as well as capacity-building missions are also discussed in the context of long-term development of states, as summarised by the key concept 'Security and Development', referring to the interplay between development and security. Understanding and mastering the transitional process from conflict to stability is difficult and perhaps the biggest challenge for academics and practitioners alike. There is a need for more research on how these new and increasingly complex as well as specialised peace operations should be carried out.

Related to this development are the non-UN led invasions (as distinct from peace operations), almost always lacking prior authorisation by the United Nations Security Council. This type of invasions has occurred on numerous occasions during the past decades and includes the US-led invasions of Grenada (1983) and Haiti (1994); the US invasion of Panama (1989); NATO's invasion of Kosovo (1999); Vietnam's invasion of Cambodia (1978); Tanzania's invasion of Uganda (1979), and a multinational (INTERFET) intervention in Timor Leste (1999); a multinational intervention in the Solomon Islands (2003), and yet another multinational intervention in Haiti (2004) (Alexander, 2000; Roberts, 2006; Heldt, 2008a). The interveners' stated rationale for these invasions included reference to humanitarian issues (e.g., safeguarding their own citizens against real or feared violence), and the goal was to oust the incumbent national or local governments. Meanwhile, only the interventions in Timor Leste, Kosovo and Haiti were succeeded by follow-up operations, here in terms of UN-led as well as non-UN-led peacekeeping operations, whereas the other operations were followed by regime change. Although carried out for stated non-humanitarian purposes, the recent non-UN authorised US-led invasions of Afghanistan (2001) and Iraq (2003) are thus part of a not uncommon phenomenon in world politics, as the invasion of Georgia by the Russian Federation in 2008. Nevertheless, a number of new challenges have arisen after these interventions in Afghanistan and Iraq, and they concern how follow-up, monitoring and stability operations endorsed by the UN/EU and supportive of the host government, as distinct from traditional and neutral peacekeeping operations, should be carried out where there is no peace to keep. This is a new role and a new challenge faced by the international community, but at the same time it is unclear whether it is a future trend.

On a final note, whereas Sweden has a long history of participation in peacekeeping, research in Sweden on the topic is, paradoxically, almost absent. At the same time, Swedish research on preventive diplomacy is showing signs of growth. The Academy welcomes more research within Sweden with a particular focus not only on preventive diplomacy, but also on peacekeeping operations. We thus look forward to increased attention by the Swedish research community to these topics.

Henrik Landerholm
Director General, Folke Bernadotte Academy

War and Peace in Transition

Karin Aggestam & Annika Björkdahl

Introduction

The last century has been referred to as the era of 'total war' in which we witnessed two world wars, the dawn of a nuclear age and superpower rivalry that polarised the world into East and West. With the end of the Cold War, expectations were raised of a more peaceful period, but new forms of violence emerged. Judging by its early years, the twenty-first century is no less conflict-prone than previous centuries. As the causes, dynamics and consequences of war have changed, so have the opportunities and efforts to establish peace. The unresolved dilemmas of the 1990s, such as humanitarian intervention and peacemaking, are joined by new dilemmas of peace-building, state reconstruction and democracy promotion. The international community needs to explore the utility of traditional strategies of conflict management and make sure to adapt them to different conflict settings. In short, the demands and challenges facing external actors in processes leading from war to peace in the twenty-first century are countless.

War in transition

War is a pervasive and universal phenomenon, yet the sheer variety of conflict types, causes, actors and dynamics is striking. The post-Cold War era has been characterised by a varied pattern of war and the emergence of new global security threats.

Changing patterns of conflict

The proportion of intrastate conflicts to interstate conflicts has grown markedly throughout the post-Second World War period (Human Security Report, 2005). Interstate wars have decreased, yet at the same time powerful states are projecting power and conducting military interventions in Afghanistan, Iraq and Georgia. In the last two decades we have seen an upsurge of conflicts, which some refer to as 'new wars' (Kaldor, 2001) or 'wars of a third kind' (Holsti, 1996). Intrastate wars have waxed and waned over recent decades and they have been unevenly distributed, with Africa and Asia experiencing more organised violence than other regions. The outbreak of secessionist war in former Yugoslavia brought intrastate war to Europe and made this phenomenon more visible as it transformed from something that occurred only in the periphery to something centre-stage.

We have also witnessed widening fractures between and among cultures and a growing cultural divide between Islam and the West. The emergence of a new form of global terrorism, as demonstrated by the 9/11 attack on the US, has changed the global security environment and the sense of insecurity has grown. Hopes for peace in the Middle East have been dashed by the escalating conflicts between Israelis and Palestinians as well as by the wars in Afghanistan and Iraq. In addition, the processes often referred to as globalisation have cemented the gap between North and South, creating tensions between those who gain and those who lose from these global processes. Scarce natural resources are at stake in many contemporary conflicts, such as the conflict in the Darfur region of Sudan. Poverty and failed states are not directly causing violent conflict or terrorism but may provide fertile ground for growing discontent and feelings of marginalization.

The developments in Iraq, Afghanistan and the Middle East demonstrate clear examples of the contemporary trend that peace and war often exist in parallel, and contemporary peace operations simultaneously involve combat operations and building peace. A state of no war – no peace is common as violence now continues during peace processes and after peace accords are agreed.

Identity conflicts

While these conflicts differ in contexts and histories, they share a number of distinct features, which make them particularly resistant to settle through negotiations and traditional diplomacy. According to some scholars, they stand in stark contrast to our traditional understanding of interstate war. Firstly, claims to power and political arguments are frequently based on identity discourses and ethnic homogeneity. Politics revolve around identity labels of community rather than ideology and national interests of states. As a consequence, it is difficult to distinguish clear strategic goals among the disputants (Kaldor, 1999: 77–78). Secondly, as these conflicts are identity-based, they draw heavily on discourses of historic enmity, hatred and insecurity, which trigger basic existential fears of group survival, expulsion and ethnic cleansing. Political legitimacy is often mobilised by using arguments from idealised nostalgic history and mythmaking.

Paradoxically, in the midst of increasing existential threats and intensified insecurity, identification provides a sense of security of being part of a larger collective (Schulz, 1999). Thirdly, these conflicts are distinct from interstate conflicts since they often take place within collapsing and weak states. The result is anarchy with an eroding norm system and state monopoly of violence. The distinction between civilians and combatants is blurred as civilians are directly targeted. Civilians therefore constitute the majority of war victims. Women and children suffer the worst consequences of these conflicts. The Democratic Republic of Congo (DRC) is a case in point, where women in the province of East Kivu are suffering from the systematic use of sexual violence as a tactic of war. Hence, any rules of warfare are rendered meaningless. In this anarchic context, warlords prove to be the major players, both as instigators of violence and paradoxically as providers of security for some groups, as we have seen in Afghanistan. Moreover, warlords in most cases profit financially from the ongoing violence, and the privatisation of violence leads to an ever-increasing number of conflicting parties and non-state actors (Kaldor, 1999).

As a consequence, these identity-driven conflicts are frequently depicted as zero-sum conflicts and are exhausting in human and material terms. Yet societies learn over time to cope and adapt to an abnormal, violent and insecure environment through various social and psychological mechanisms, which is one of several reasons why some of these conflicts become intractable. In intractable conflicts, such as the one in Israel-Palestine, the parties have accumulated and institutionalised discourses of hatred, prejudice and animosity towards the other. Collective memories and national myths also play a significant role in the reconstruction of self and enemy images. These perceptions turn into an 'ideology' that supports the prolongation of conflict and serves as an identity marker of who we are/who we are not, and thus tends to be resistant to change. As a consequence, the vicious and self-perpetuating circles of violence are 'normalised' and become central to everyday life (Bar-Tal, 2001).

Continuities and discontinuities

While recognising changes and new challenges, evidence also points to important continuities in war and peace. Many of the sources of conflict that occurred in the 1990s and in previous epochs, for example, the security dilemma, state failure, economic predation, political transitions and ethnic tensions, remain valid and relevant today. Regional stability continues to be compromised by those conflicts that last over time and are largely intractable, for example Israel-Palestine, Sudan, North Korea and Jammu Kashmir. Many of these conflicts have refused to yield despite repeated peacemaking efforts and rounds of mediation. They are a major source of international instability because of the risk that they may escalate. When addressing violent conflicts and designing strategies for conflict prevention, management and resolution, we need to keep in mind both factors of continuity and drivers of change.

At the same time, there has been a decrease in the number of wars, of episodes of mass killing, and of people dying violent battle deaths in the last two decades, despite the terrible cases of Rwanda, former Yugoslavia, and the ongoing conflicts in the DRC, Somalia, Sudan and elsewhere. Another positive and unnoticed development is the reduction in violent conflict in sub-Saharan Africa where the combat toll has dropped. But they are only a small part of the whole story of the suffering from war. In general, 90% or more of war-related deaths are due to disease and malnutrition rather than direct violence, as we have seen, for example, in the Congo and Darfur. The single most compelling explanation for these positive changes is found in the unprecedented upsurge of international activism, spearheaded by the UN in the wake of the Cold War (Human Security Report, 2005).

However, there are troubling signs that international norms and institutions, which upheld human rights, established codes of conduct in war, checked the proliferation of nuclear weapons, banned landmines and deterred piracy are eroding in many corners of the world. At the same time, support for democratisation processes are included in many of the United Nations mandates for peace support operations and an international consensus is growing in support of the emerging norm pertaining to the responsibility to protect (R2P), aimed at protecting civilians from mass atrocities (Evans, 2008). These emerging norms challenge or may provide alternative interpretations of the institutionalised norm of state sovereignty, which guides interstate relations and limits the possibilities for external actors to interfere in the domestic affairs of states.

Peacemaking in transition

Peace is elusive and the quest for peace is perpetual. Yet in response to the transformation of war, efforts to promote and build peace have been transformed. Peace operations, for example, have moved away from traditional peacekeeping to complex peace support operations. These new types of multifunctional, multidimensional and complex peace operations have an ambitious agenda, ranging from conflict prevention to state reconstruction and peacebuilding.

Forces for good

At times, the use of military force by external parties is required to stop violence, establish security and stability and prevent relapse into war. This form of coercive diplomacy remains a controversial option in peace operations and is often the last resort. Yet the appropriate and timely use of force can make a difference in preventing the outbreak of massive violence or in bringing the parties to the negotiation table.

However, the use of force alone does not bring peace. It needs to be accompanied by a political process of peacemaking, including mediation and negotiation. Other civilian, humanitarian and policing tasks are also required. Most conflict situations are defined as complex humanitarian emergencies with displaced people and massive starvation, requiring support for relief aid and refugee camps, safe havens, humanitarian corridors, humanitarian emergency assistance and assistance for refugee return. To create stability and a secure environment, security sector reform (SSR) and demobilisation, disarmament and reintegration (DDR) are crucial. The availability of light weapons and small arms in most conflict zones in combination with unemployed, demobilised former combatants are obvious threats to stability. It increases violence in the form of criminal violence, which threatens everyday lives and the process towards peace in many war-torn societies. Conflict-ridden societies also frequently lack sufficient institutional capacity, and reconstructing state institutions has become a major task following the peace operations. The international community is also often involved in promoting new norms and practices pertaining to good governance, peaceful conflict resolution, democracy, rule of law and human rights.

Privatisation of peacemaking

Another general trend, which to a certain extent may be viewed as part of the liberal peacebuilding model, is the privatisation of peacemaking. As many contemporary conflicts concern state-society relations, NGOs come to play an increasing and vital role in peacemaking. Duffield (1997), for example, argues that economic development is becoming the West's favoured response to 'new' wars. Economic development has become 'securitised' and part of the general framework of conflict management, conflict prevention and peacemaking. At the same time, NGOs are today significant actors in economic development, particularly in the last decades as the West's official development assistance (ODA) in general has seen major cutbacks and/or has been relocated to NGOs. This trend of 'privatisation' is partly based on the assumption that development assistance will become more efficient. Activities by NGOs are believed to be more participatory, flexible, innovative and effective, while less expensive than governmental agencies. For example, it is seen as easier for NGOs than for governmental agencies to link development aid to ethnic reconciliation. Moreover, these activities are seen as contributing to the growth of civil society and good governance, which will prevent future conflicts. In other words, there seems to be an 'agreeable fit' between the privatisation of ODA and NGOs (Duffield, 1997; Nicolaidis, 1995: 60–64). Also, many states are 'contracting' out humanitarian relief and assistance to NGOs.

This trend of 'privatisation' of world politics in general and diplomacy in particular tends on the one hand to de-politicise peacemaking, which ultimately is value-laden. The activities of NGOs are often framed as apolitical tools in the management of conflict, particularly in disputes where states are seen as the inhibitors of socio-economic development. Hence, the 'de-politicisation' of NGOs risks focusing on technical and not political solutions. However, others argue in contrast that the trend of privatisation of peacemaking is part of a policy agenda of neo-liberal economics and liberal peacebuilding. NGOs, by this interpretation, come to symbolise everything that governments are not; that is, unburdened with large bureaucracies, flexible and open to innovations, faster at implementing development efforts and quicker to respond to grass roots needs (Duffield, 1997; Natsios, 1995: 444–446).

The new actors in security, ranging from international peacekeepers to private actors such as military security companies, attempt to fill the security vacuum and provide the security the state fails to uphold, and development agents, such as NGOs, attempt to meet the demands for food, shelter and health unmet in weak and failed states. This contributes to a privatisation of both security and the state, which obscures the public-private distinction. In addition, state security has partly been replaced by the notion of human security, prioritising the security of the individual before the security of the state, and aims to ensure freedom from want and freedom from fear.

Coordination and cooperation

The sheer number of actors involved in various peace efforts makes coordination and cooperation between states, intergovernmental organisations (IGO) and NGOs critical. How workable such cooperation is depends largely on the existence of some kind of shared understanding of war and peace in general. Furthermore, they need to pool resources and improve coordination in order to meet the challenging task of preventing and managing contemporary conflicts, which are bound to be at the core of the twenty-first century of diplomacy. Some describe this (inter)governmental–NGO relationship as one more of convenience than of a 'passionate romance'. Each side remains distrustful and uncomfortable about working together, partly because they differ (and at times compete) in their understandings of peace, as well as speaking to different constituencies (Natsios, 1995: 413). There are, for example, many governments which regard information emanating from NGOs as inaccurate and unbalanced because they are considered to have their own agendas, which do not conform to the views held by many diplomats. This 'credibility problem' becomes particularly troubling at times of early warning issued by NGOs (Carnegie Commission, 1997: 10).

Yet the diverse roles and activities of NGOs often take place in parallel or together with states and IGOs. The advantages of NGOs are that they are grass root-centred and close to the field and thus come to play important roles in diplomacy, particularly in the early phases of conflict through early warning and in the post-conflict phase. NGOs may, for example, facilitate through 'soft mediation' communication channels, foster peaceful dialogues between disputing parties and counter hate propaganda (Nicolaidis, 1995: 60–65). In addition, MacFarquhar, Rotberg, Chen (1995: 6) suggest that 'field diplomacy' should be further developed, which means sending NGO teams to regions of antagonism for extended periods of time in order to stimulate and support local initiatives for peace-building. Also, a growing number of human rights missions have become integral parts of second/third generations of peacekeeping in post-conflict settings. These are also referred to as multifunctional peacekeeping, which includes features of traditional peacekeeping, but concerns larger international deployments, with a wider mandate and greater non-military dimensions.

In short, the enormous challenges of contemporary efforts to ensure durable peace require cooperation by a multitude of various actors and create problems of coordination. The division of labour is often unclear and lead agencies are not always designated. In general, there is a need for collaboration between civilian and military actors, between state and non-state actors, between external and internal actors, and between the elite and the general population. Obviously, coordination and cooperation are major challenges to complex peace missions and few principles have been agreed upon to establish reasonable burden-sharing, efficient division of labour and legitimate leadership in order to avoid overlap, competition and inefficient use of scarce resources.

Chronic conflicts resistant to peace efforts

Despite international and domestic efforts, emerging conflicts have resisted efforts at prevention and in many post-conflict societies peace processes have reached impasse or collapsed. On other occasions, a frustrated and contested peace has emerged from the peace processes, where the peace is constantly challenged and threatened by a relapse into violence. Instead of promoting a self-sustainable peace, external peace-builders have at best managed to freeze an emerging conflict while the root causes of the conflict are still largely unaddressed. In other cases an ambivalent peace has been established in the aftermath of violent conflict. Both situations are recognised by the absence of large-scale violence, but with persistent inter-communal insecurity, discrimination of out-group members and where ethno-national groups continue to face societal security dilemmas. This in turn means that there exists only weak popular legitimacy for the existing peace (Kostic, 2008: 95). This has spurred research towards a more critical direction and assessment of peacebuilding strategies, particularly focusing on the poor record of successful implementation and durability of peace agreements (Stedman *et al.* 2002; Hampson, 1996). Although every peacebuilding situation has its own dynamics, a lesson to be drawn from the many mistakes in the last decades is that leaving too soon, or doing too little, are the most common mistakes rather than staying too long or doing too much. At the same time, all intrusive peace operations need an exit strategy, and one that is more comprehensive than just holding elections as soon as possible.

The quest for peace

The peace that follows many contemporary conflicts is often unsatisfactory and marked by a continuation of inter-ethnic tensions, lack of order and eruption of violence. The lack of sustainable peace arrangements is illuminated in the body of literature, which conceptualises peace as temporary and contested in terms of fragile, precarious, unstable, or turbulent peace. In this vein, the liberal democratic peace has emerged as the dominant idea for a sustainable peace. The liberal democratic peace promises to deliver reconciliation and reconstruction in post-war societies. This notion of peace has been widely promoted as a means of coming to terms with many of the problems facing unsuccessful peace processes. It is based on peaceful conflict resolution, protection of human rights and minority rights, political representation, good governance and rule of law. In theory, it may also emancipate individuals. Both the elite delivering the peace and the grass roots receiving it become acculturated to the liberal democratic peace idea (MacGinty, 2006). As the liberal democratic peace is perceived as superior to alternative understandings of peace, little space is left during the negotiations to explore local varieties of peace and to incorporate local articulations of peace. Consequently, rival notions of peace are not put forward in peace processes and thus peace accords will rarely reflect local understandings of peace. Challenging conventional wisdom, MacGinty argues that 'the peace delivered on behalf of the liberal democratic peace is often illiberal and undemocratic' (MacGinty, 2006: 35). Although a bad peace is better than no peace, the quality of peace should be critically examined. Johan Galtung's two concepts of positive and negative peace can here assist in assessing the outcome of various peacemaking efforts.

Challenges for external actors

To be sure, these distinct transformative features of war and peace lead to a number of challenges to peacemaking and interventions by external actors. We have identified four such challenges which are particularly troublesome for external actors to resolve when pursuing peacemaking: (1) recognition and the problem of compromise, (2) asymmetry and the problem of mediation entry, (3) spoiling behaviour and the problem of managing violence, and (4) implementation and the problem of compliance.

Recognition and compromise

First, negotiations are often stalled because recognition needs to be resolved before any meaningful progress can be made. As the negotiations involve a multitude of actors and non-state actors, recognition, legitimacy and leadership become decisive and major issues of contention in a peace process. Hence, how to deal with the large number of factional parties in a negotiation process is a major challenge for external actors. For example, who is to be considered a valid spokesperson and a legitimate leader of a non-state actor? Who are to be included and excluded in the process? What are the consequences of exclusion? John Darby (2001: 118–119) argues for a 'sufficient inclusion,' which includes those with power to bring the peace process down by violence, such as militant organisations.

Non-state actors on the one hand dispute their lack of recognised status, and governments on the other hand dispute claims for proto-political status (Richmond, 2006: 66–68). Recognition is therefore often withheld either as a way to undermine the other side's position or simply because it does not benefit the long-term interest of oneself. Consequently, the principle of negotiating in good faith becomes increasingly problematic since compromise is secondary to recognition and legitimacy. In many cases, peace negotiations are initiated after heavy international pressures are exerted on the parties. The parties may hold devious objectives and accept negotiations for other reasons than compromise (Richmond, 1997). Hence, a major challenge is therefore how to establish good-faith negotiations which are based on the commitment, good intention and willingness of the parties to reach a mutually satisfying agreement that will be honoured. Frequently, parties may use a peace and negotiation process primarily as a way to gain legitimacy and recognition. Compromise and reaching an agreement may thus be secondary for the disputants.

Furthermore, many contemporary conflicts are, as mentioned above, identity-based and therefore particularly difficult to resolve via negotiations. Negotiations are framed as a zero-sum game and as major risk-taking since compromises involve existential questions and concerns of group survival. The role of religion as part of the identity construction and justification of violence exacerbates the difficulties of conducting negotiations based on compromise. Religion is about absolute and particularistic values. Hence, political goals become less visible and incentives to compromise are limited at best or non-existing at worst. The existential framing of negotiation, in combination with uncertainty about the direction of a peace process, feeds mistrust and fear. Also a negotiation process by itself may challenge the disputants' sense of understanding 'self' and 'other', which is intimately related to conflict. Thus, belief perseverance is further strengthened if there is a continuation of violence. It proves that the other side has not changed and consequently confirms firmly held enemy images.

Asymmetry and mediation

The asymmetry that characterises most contemporary conflicts is considered by most negotiation theorists as detrimental to efficient mediation and negotiation. As William Zartman (1995: 8) states, 'negotiations under conditions of asymmetry (asymmetrical negotiations) are a paradox, because one of the basic findings about the negotiation process is that it functions best under conditions of equality.' Consequently, implications of asymmetry in a negotiation process are numerous (see further, Aggestam, 2002). Moreover, asymmetry makes a continuation of unilateral actions more likely. Hence, a mutually hurting stalemate, which William Zartman (1989) defines as a particularly ripe moment for mediation and negotiation, becomes less probable. Such a stalemate stipulates increasing symmetrical relations and a situation where the parties are trapped, without being able to resort to unilateral strategies. However, asymmetrical conflicts are characterised by gross power inequality in economic, political and military resources between state and non-state actors. Stronger parties are inclined to use their power superiority to continue unilateral actions, whereas weaker parties mobilise strength and compensate for the asymmetry through strongly held commitments to the armed resistance (Zartman, 1995: 9).

When delineating the characteristics of asymmetrical conflict, it becomes evident what an immense challenge it is for mediators to gain acceptance and legitimacy for intervention. Mediators face several specific problems. There is a discrepancy in the expectations of mediation between strong and weak parties. Strong parties tend to reject international mediation, whereas weak parties make constant appeals for forceful international intervention. Strong parties may therefore put a number of preconditions, which the mediators and the weak parties have to accept in order to get the negotiation process started. Consequently, stronger parties tend to stipulate the 'rules of negotiation'. Moreover, since stronger parties exhibit lesser political willingness to negotiate, mediators are particularly attentive to their positions in conflicts. Furthermore, mediation may be used by parties who are not committed to negotiations and compromises. Mediation therefore becomes a cover for more 'devious objectives', such as to enhance international legitimacy or gain time, as discussed above. Mediation may also be used simply to preserve a status quo situation in the conflict without the parties attempting to resolve it. The conflicting parties might also be inclined to focus their efforts to allying with the mediators rather than creating common grounds with the opposing party (Richmond, 1998; 1999).

Spoiler management

In recent years the spoiling problem has gained increasing attention among external actors. Spoiling refers to intentional acts of violence aimed at derailing a peace process. Yet in academia it is a relatively unexplored area of research. Stephen Stedman (1997), who introduced the notion of spoiler and spoiling, has contributed with important research, particularly on policy-relevant issues regarding the role of international custodians. Also the work by John Darby (2001) and together with Robert MacGinty (2003) has generated important insights about the impact of violence during peace processes, deduced from a large number of empirical case studies (see also Newman & Richmond, 2006). Even though peacemaking is highly complex, divisive and uncertain in its outcome, the spoiler problem paradoxically tends to be a predictable phenomenon in most contemporary peace processes. Paul Pillar (1983) also underlines that most peace negotiations are accompanied by ongoing violence.

A peace process almost by definition produces spoiling behaviour since it challenges established assumptions of who is a patriot and traitor, enemy and friend. Who become the winner and loser when a peace agreement is to be implemented? One decisive factor is leadership, that is, the ability of political leaders to deliver their followers and manage groups associated with violence. Political leaders will have difficulties leading if their followers are unwilling to go in the same direction (Darby, 2001: 121). Moreover, leaders who sign agreements are vulnerable to accusations of betrayal and treason, which often work as a powerful deterrent against those who want to promote a peaceful settlement with the enemy (Iklé, 1964: 60). Violence in such circumstances will feed existing fears and uncertainties among the general public about the direction of the peace process. Opposition groups may convincingly argue that compromises do not lead to peace, but to more violence (rewarding and giving in to terror), which limits the mandate and bargaining range of the negotiators. Spoiling is particularly effective when political leaders have publicly declared and made a commitment not to negotiate and make concessions under fire. It is assumed that to negotiate while violence continues signals weakness to the other side, even though in practice it means that the negotiators become hostages to spoilers. Hence, spoilers become the veto-holders of the peace process and determine its pace and direction (Darby, 2001: 118).

The power of spoiler groups is further enhanced when extremists on both sides, despite their violent struggle against each other, tend to form a tacit alliance where they can derive justification from each other (Aggestam & Jönsson, 1997: 778–80). As Andrew Kydd and Barbara Walter (2002: 264) underline, 'extremists are surprisingly successful in bringing down peace processes if they so desire'. For instance, only 25% of signed peace accords in civil wars between 1988 and 1998 were implemented due to violence taking place during negotiations (Kydd & Walter, 2002: 264). Hence, the capacity of spoilers to undermine a negotiation process depends on the degree of popular support they enjoy among the public as well as on their principled stance to continue an armed and violent struggle. Some spoilers, whom Stephen Stedman refers to as total spoilers (in contrast to greedy and limited spoilers), simply cannot be accommodated or defeated since their demands are non-negotiable. The popular support of spoilers also depends on how the public view the peace process in general and how active or passive war and peace constituencies are. Yet as John Darby (2001: 98) soberly points out, peace negotiations rarely result from domestic pressures, despite years of war-weariness.

Stephen Stedman (1996: 350) underlines the complex transition for leaders, who were previously committed to the rhetoric of total war and victory, to enter into a negotiation process and declare willingness to conduct compromise. Since leaders in such circumstances may be accused of cowardice and treachery, they may out of fear talk peace in private and war in public. Secret negotiations are therefore often sought to avoid arousing public anxiety despite the fact that secrecy is generally seen as democratically offensive. The sheer fact of being excluded from the process may therefore generate opposition and spoiling. If the negotiations are surrounded by violence and viewed as unjust and illegitimate, concession-making and implementation of an agreement become almost impossible.

Implementation and compliance

The problem of implementation is a widespread dilemma in most contemporary peace processes. The reasons are many and varied. International law specifically states that *pacta sunt servanda*, but enforcement mechanisms are often absent in many peace agreements. However, custodian monitoring has become more frequent in recent years. Custodians are, according to Stephen Stedman (1997), international actors who oversee the implementation of peace agreements. For example, in Cambodia the United Nations has acted as a custodian and the United Kingdom and Ireland as joint 'internal' custodians of the Northern Ireland peace process. Other obstacles to implementation may be that the agreements have been badly designed, vaguely defined, or intentionally ambiguous since the parties have relied on constructive ambiguity[1] as a way of avoiding deadlocks (Hampson, 1996). It may exacerbate an already fragile situation characterised by suspicion and mistrust, and consequently create new grounds for hostilities because these ambiguities need to be addressed, interpreted and agreed upon. A 'sceptical scrutiny' of a peace agreement may develop and as a result there is a reactive devaluation of the agreement (Ross, 1997: 34). In such cases, third parties may play a monitoring role in promoting new norms and codes of conduct, particularly in the area of human rights and minority rights. They may report on misbehaviour and investigate human rights abuses and other war crimes. Amnesty International, Human Rights Watch and the Organisation of Security and Cooperation in Europe play such roles.

---

1 'Constructive ambiguity' is a frequently used diplomatic term. The intention is to overcome deadlocks by avoiding and postponing detailed interpretations until implementation. The basic rationale is that the parties will be more committed to a signed agreement, that is, following the device of *pacta sunt servanda*. However, in identity-based conflicts, which often lack established or accepted rules of the game of negotiation, constructive ambiguity frequently turns destructive and counterproductive.

Outline of the book

Chapter one examines the role of private military and security companies and discusses their engagement in contemporary conflicts under the 'culture of impunity.' Anna Leander explores the complexity of international legal and regulatory tools to regulate the activities of these actors. The second chapter examines the link between the privatisation of security in the context of armed conflict and state control of force. Joakim Berndtsson provides an empirical analysis of the changes and challenges of the privatisation of security in Iraq. Chapter three presents an overview of the European Union's efforts of conflict resolution in the Israeli-Palestinian conflict. Michael Schultz pays particular attention to the political visions, ambitions and strategies of the EU directed at the level of the political elite, middle and grassroots level. Chapter four, by Kersti Larsdotter, assesses the changes and challenges in peace operations concerning the use of military force at the tactical level of operation. She argues that the conduct of military force has a crucial impact on the outcome of peace operations. In the fifth chapter, Maria Småberg utilises a historical perspective to challenge the conventional understanding that women are new in the peacebuilding arena. She provides a historical account of the Swedish missionary and peacebuilder Alma Johansson, an eyewitness to the Armenian genocide, and explores the role of women in peacebuilding. In chapter six, Birger Heldt raises questions about the sequencing of various peacemaking efforts, such as when mediation should be undertaken in violent conflicts to ensure cumulative as well as synergetic effects. Chapter seven explores the mediation efforts of Norway in the Sri Lankan peace process. Kristine Höglund and Isak Svensson analyse among other things the motivation behind mediation initiatives. The book[2] concludes with a summary by the editors, highlighting some of the challenges faced by external actors engaged in the transition from war to peace.

---

2 This book is a result of the biannual conference on Peace and Conflict Research, which was held at Lund University in October 2008. Financial support for organising this event was graciously granted by the Folke Bernadotte Academy. Thanks also to David Ratford, who provided excellent proof reading of the manuscript.

CHAPTER I

New Roles for External Actors?

Disagreements about International Regulation of Private Armies

Anna Leander

Introduction

Private Military and Security Companies (PMSCs) are increasingly visible and controversial. Public discussion about how these companies should be regulated is particularly intense. The Blackwater killing of 17 civilians on 16 September 2007 in Nisour Square, Baghdad, has come to epitomize the issue. However, the problem of regulation runs deeper and is more complex than the scapegoating of Blackwater, which focuses on the killing of civilians in Iraq and the ensuing legal process. It spans not only accountability for violations of human rights norms, but also accountability in the economic, social and political sphere. Moreover, it has deep roots in the contemporary neoliberal governance practices, which makes accountability exceedingly difficult.

This chapter does not deal with all the complexities tied to the issue of what amounts to nothing less than a 'culture of impunity'

Acknowledgement. This chapter has grown out of a policy statement presented to UN working groups at the Latin America and Caribbean Regional Consultation on the Effects of the Activities of Private Military and Security Companies on the Enjoyment of Human Rights: Regulation and Oversight, Panama, 17–18 December 2007. I would like to thank the working group for the opportunity to develop these thoughts, for its input, and also to acknowledge the support of the *Hanse Wissenschafts Kolleg* in Delmenhorst where I wrote the original version of this text. I would also like to thank the participants of the National Conference Peace and Conflict Research in Lund (2–3 October 2008) for their comments.

benefitting PMSCs (Leander, 2007a; Human Rights First, 2008). Although this chapter will hint at some of these wider issues, it will deal in detail only with one sub-question about accountability, namely the question of whether or not it is necessary to expand international regulation and assign new roles to external actors to regulate private military and security companies (PMSCs)[1].

Contradictory and seemingly incompatible answers to this question abound. While there is a general consensus that regulation needs to be improved, there is little clarity about what this means. On the one hand, it is often suggested that there is a lack of regulation and that PMSCs operate in a legal vacuum. Thus, what we need is ultimately more international regulation and new roles for external actors (Bailes & Holmqvist, 2007; Singer, 2007b). On the other side of the argument, these assertions are confronted by statements underlining that PMSCs are covered by international law and therefore do not operate in an international vacuum. The problem is rather the multiplicity of contradictory legal norms and standards and too many external regulators, whose numbers should be reduced and roles clarified (Scoville, 2006; Zarate, 1998; Doswald-Beck, 2007). This chapter argues that both positions are partly valid. A multiplicity of indirect international legal instruments coexists with a scarcity of specific ones. But more centrally, it argues that the focus on whether or not there is a regulatory vacuum distracts attention from the more fundamental question of what regulation should be about. On this question disagreement is profound, but well masked by the mantra that we need to improve regulation. This chapter maps the key positions in this disagreement.

In order to make this dual point, the chapter departs from the complexity and diversity of PMSC activity as an object of international regulation. This clarifies the abundance of potentially relevant *indirect* international instruments of regulation, as well as the scarcity of international instruments *specifically* designed to regulate PMSCs. The chapter then proceeds to suggest that while

---

1 A PMSC is a company that provides goods and services that have a military character, whether or not they do so in a formal situation of peace and hence only provide 'security' in a situation of war. Details are given in section 2.

the technical difficulties of using this specific constellation of legal instruments may be part of the explanation, the main reason is that states have not been interested in using them and/or in promoting the development of more effective regulation. Ultimately the reason for this is that they have profoundly diverging views on what regulation should be for. The last section maps the key positions in this disagreement. The last two points are made using the United Nations (UN) 1989 Convention against the Finance and Use of Mercenaries as an example.

PMSC: A complex object of regulation

When regulation is discussed it is important to clarify what it is one wants to regulate, why, how and at what cost. A look at what PMSCs do, in what contexts and what kind of things they are, makes clear that no self-evident simple answer can be given to these questions. As the scale and scope of private military and security companies are rapidly expanding internationally, the question of their regulation is ever more pressing. Although credible, exact figures on the activities of the companies are not available,[2] there is ample indication that the companies play a central role around the world. In Iraq, a Department of Defense survey estimates that there are some 180 000 contractors compared to 160 000 US troops (Singer, 2007a: 2). In Nigeria some 1000 registered security companies constitute the second economic sector in the economy after oil (Abrahamsen & Williams, 2006a). Moreover, the scope of PMSC activity is steadily expanding. The trend to privatise and outsource a growing range of activities places PMSCs in charge of an ever-growing range of formerly military or policing tasks.

PMSCs have in common that they are private firms selling military and security services. However, this covers a wide range of things.[3]

---

2 I endorse the IPOA suggestion that 'current information about the Private Security Industry is largely piecemeal and unsubstantiated', something the organization's 'industry survey' (based on 14 companies) does not address (IPOA, 2007).

3 For detailed introductions to the industry and its activities see (Singer, 2003;

PMSCs are firms involved in the provision of logistics, such as cooking, construction work, medical services, but also the provision and maintenance of equipment including armament systems, in-air refuelling of military aircraft or the operation of UAVs (unmanned armed vehicles). They also do consultancy advising on security needs, often involving suggestions for how to answer those needs, including in situations of armed conflict. Their tasks may include training of armed forces, police units, and private security staff that may place contractors in actual conflict situations. Intelligence may include the provision, analysis and suggestions for measures to be taken. Finally, PMSCs provide direct security services, such as the guarding of convoys, of military compounds and of refugee camps, as well as provision of personnel for specific security or military operations. Clearly, these activities at times make some PMSCs assume military tasks.

More than this, it is useful to recall that PMSCs work in diverse contexts and for a variety of clients. PMSCs work spans the full range of contexts. In particular, it is worth recalling that PMSCs operate in political situations ranging from declared war, internal wars, and post-conflict situations to more stable and peaceful phases. They are present in geographical locations spanning stable, developed OECD states (e.g. Germany) as well as highly unstable states with severe and lasting security problems (e.g. Kivu). PMSCs work for clients including public armed forces and states, but also political movements, private firms, NGOs, criminal organisations and private individuals. Lastly, the legality of PMSC contracts ranges from the fully illegal contract (e.g. an organised crime organisation hiring a security specialist to bomb a rival), to contracts that are partially legal (e.g. states using PMSCs to do their 'dirty work'), to contracts that are fully legal (e.g. a registered contract between an extractive firm and a contractor guarding its installations).

Finally, firms referred to as PMSCs are very diverse. They are of varying size and stability. Some firms are large multinational corporations, quoted on stock-markets with long corporate histories, while others are informal one-man creations that come and go. They are

Avant, 2005; Leander, 2006).

also of varying origin. PMSCs are often talked and written about as if they were only or mainly a UK and US phenomenon. It may be worth recalling that this is not the case. A Kenyan company, KK, for example, is widely present in East Africa, and companies across Latin America, Africa and Asia have subcontracted staff to firms in Iraq and Afghanistan. PMSCs have varying ties to their home states and to public security forces. Some firms are closely tied to their home states and to armed forces while others operate largely independently. Last but not least, the companies have varying company cultures/policies and strategies on issues such as the vetting of staff, labour relations, choice of clients, and acceptable working environments/tasks.

No international legal vacuum

Because the activities of PMSCs are diverse, complex and multiple, they raise correspondingly multiple and complex legal and regulatory questions. Making a complete list of these questions and the legal instruments that might be used to address them is far beyond the ambition of this chapter. Rather, the purpose below is to make the point that there is an abundance of international legal instruments indirectly relevant for the regulation of this activity. At the same time, there is certainly a near legal vacuum of instruments directly conceived to regulate PMSCs (see table 1 for an overview). This makes clear how and why lawyers (and others) seem able to advance such contradictory claims with regard to the state of PMSC regulation under international law, claiming both over- and under-regulation. But more significantly, this is a first step in making clear that focusing the discussion about the role of international law and external actors on the existence or not of legal instruments is likely to be misleading.

Some PMSC activity falls directly under the international regulation of war. The International Committee of the Red Cross (ICRC) has insisted, repeatedly that when PMSCs work in armed conflicts they are no less subject to the Geneva Conventions than are other actors. The ICRC has recently contributed to the elaboration of the 'Montreux Document' (2008) (suggesting best practices for states) reaffirming this position. Because PMSCs may be used to prepare or engage in war, their activities may be subjected to restrictions as part of attempts to regulate just reasons for going to war, *jus ad bellum*. Hence, neutrality laws – as specified e.g. by the 1907 Hague Convention V (article 4) – strictly limit the role that might be played by individuals and companies of purportedly neutral states. Similarly, because PMSCs may work in war situations they are subject to the rules regulating behaviour in war, the *jus in bello*. When PMSCs engage as combatants they are bound by the Geneva Conventions and states are responsible for ensuring that these are followed. Finally, contractors are also significantly held by IHL in post-conflict situations (UCHL, 2005; UN, 2005).

Slightly more specifically, part of PMSC activity falls under the international regulation of mercenarism. It does so to the extent that PMSCs engage in mercenarism as defined by international law, that is, act as soldiers of fortune.[4] The OAU Convention for the elimination of mercenarism in Africa and the UN Convention against the finance and use of mercenaries both demand that signatories refrain from using mercenaries and take measures to prevent them from operating from their territories. Even more specifically, the wide variety of PMSC activity may make a wide range of international treaties relevant for their behaviour. The list in table 1 is only a selection of treaties and conventions that have recently been invoked in relation to PMSC activities. Theoretically the list could be extended much further.

---

4 Article 47 of the protocol additional to the Geneva Conventions of 12 August 1949 spells out the definition of mercenary that the subsequent legislation is modelled on. According to this definition, a mercenary is a person who (1) is specifically recruited locally or abroad in order to fight in an armed conflict; (2) takes direct part in hostilities; (3) is motivated essentially by private gain; (4) is neither a national of a party to the conflict nor a resident of territory controlled by a party to the conflict; (5) is not a member of the armed forces of a party to the conflict; and (6) has not been sent by a state which is not a party to the conflict on official duty as a member of its armed forces.

Table 1: International Regulatory Instruments (selected examples)

	Specific	Indirect
Formal	Situation Specific Regulation: (CPA Order 17 of 24 June 2007)	**Regulation of Peace and War** – Hague Convention V – International Humanitarian Law (Geneva Conventions, additional protocols) – International Law Commission Draft Code of Offences against Peace and Security of Mankind **Regulation of Mercenarism** – 1977 OAU Convention for the Elimination of Mercenarism in Africa – 1989 UN Convention against the Finance and Use of Mercenaries **Specialised Treaties/Conventions** – The UN Convention against Transnational Organized Crime – The UN Convention against Torture – The Slavery Convention – Council of Europe Convention on Action against Trafficking – ILO Conventions – Tokyo Convention on Offences and Certain Other Acts Committed on Board Aircraft – Hague Convention for the Suppression of Unlawful Seizure of Aircraft – Convention in the Prevention and Punishment of Crimes against Internationally Protected Persons – Convention against the Taking of Hostages

		– Convention for the Suppression of Unlawful Acts against the Safety of Maritime Navigation – The UN Mine Action Standards Arms Trade Regulations: – ECOWAS Convention on Small Arms and Light Weapons – EU Arms Export Controls, embargoes – UN Small Arms Trade Treaty Internationally applied national legislations – the US Foreign and Corrupt Practices Act – the UK Anti-Terrorism, Crime and Security Act
Informal	IPOA code of conduct BAPSC charter Voluntary Standard (e.g. The Standards (e.g. Voluntary Principles on Principles on Security and Human Rights) Firm Policies	Global Compact Standards The Code of Conduct of the International Red Cross and Red Crescent Red Crescent NGO Standards and Codes of Conduct

In addition to this, regional and international regulation of arms trade and military assistance may have a bearing on PMSC activities. Firms providing logistics, training, consultancy or providing direct security services are separated only by a thin and often blurred line from military services. Hence both more permanent rules, such as the UN Small Arms Trade Treaty, regulations of the European Union (EU) and Economic Community of West African States (ECOWAS), as well as regulations concerning a specific country or a specific conflict (embargoes of different kinds), directly regulate PMSC activity. Moreover, some regulation, which is national in origin, is adhered to internationally by firms that are not operating in the jurisdiction where the regulation is directly applicable. This is the case, for example, of the US Foreign Corrupt Practices Act or the UK anti-terrorism legislation.

Last but not least, a long list of informal rules, which have a bearing on the regulation of PMSC activities, could be addressed. Voluntary codes of conduct directly concern the activities of many PMSCs. This is true of codes of conduct that cover different aspects of company relations with the society in which they operate, with the government in the countries where they work (e.g. Transparency International Business Principles for Countering Bribery), as well as general codes of conduct regulating business behaviour in relation to specific issues (e.g. the maintenance of security[5]) or in specific sectors (e.g. the Extractive Industries Transparency Initiative) or a combination of these (e.g. UN Global Compact Principles).

This protracted and yet incomplete list of indirect international regulatory instruments underlies the view of those who argue that PMSCs are well covered by international law (e.g. de Wolf, 2007; Doswald-Beck, 2007; UCHL, 2005; Zarate, 1998). The abundance of international legal instruments indirectly relevant for the regulation of PMSC activity is matched by the paucity of instruments designed specifically to regulate PMSCs. This paucity has the same roots as the abundance of indirect instruments of regulation. The complexity, multiplicity and variety of PMSC activity have limited

---

5 The *Voluntary Principles on Security and Human Rights* for firms in extractive and energy, are a good example (www.voluntaryprinciples.org).

the development of specific international instruments for regulating PMSC activity.

There is at present no international treaty or convention that regulates the activities of PMSCs specifically. It is sometimes suggested that situation-specific regulation constitutes a form of international regulation. For example, order 17 (June 24, 2004) of the Coalition Provisional Authority (CPA) in Iraq defined the legal status of contractors working for the armed forces in Iraq. It was often interpreted as having granted contractors immunity from legal pursuit by Iraqi authorities until it was explicitly altered in 2008. However, the CPA is not an international authority and PMSC activities are not only restricted to work for public armed forces, but include work done for a wide array of businesses, aid organisations, private individuals and state agencies.

In addition, informal international regulation (or 'soft law') of PMSC activities exists in the form of limited and voluntary codes of conduct and standards of behaviour developed specifically for PMSCs. Examples of such codes of conduct include those promoted by the professional associations of companies in the sector, such as the International Peace Operations Association Code of Conduct, or the British Association of Private Security Companies Charter[6]or the Codes of Conduct. In addition to the fact that many lawyers would consider this kind of regulation as falling outside the law, it is certainly selective in the sense that voluntary codes of conduct are indeed voluntary; that is, firms can decide to adhere or not.

As this shows, PMSC activities in general are not consistently regulated by international law. The only formal form of regulation that is a consistent part of PMSC activity internationally, unless it is outright illegal, is the regulation specified in the contracts tied to specific operations. Contracts usually define the scope and scale of activities the PMSC may engage in. In conflict and war situations they also define the extent to which force may be used – the 'rules of engagement' – and/or their specific responsibilities and tasks in relation to the use of force. Contractual regulation is probably at present the formal regulation of most immediate

---

6 These are available on the association websites.

general relevance for the regulation of PMSC activity. This makes it justified to suggest, as many observers do, that PMSCs operate in a legal vacuum with regard to international law (Dorn & Levi, 2007a; Coleman, 2004; Minow, 2003; Scoville, 2006). However, as the previous discussion has illustrated, if one takes the abundance of indirect instruments relevant to PMSC activity, it is clear that those who claim that the industry is overregulated with a jungle of potentially relevant legal instruments are also right. In fact, one might doubt if regulation through international law of PMSCs in general is at all possible given the complexity of PMSC activities. Precisely because their activities cut across so many domains of international law, the most promising avenue may indeed be a mixture of using existing regulatory instruments and relying on informal soft law that is often regulating a specific area of activities within which PMSC activities may fall (as suggested by the Montreux Document). The question this in turn raises is whether this can be effective.

The limited role of international legal instruments

The record so far of using existing international law to regulate PMSCs is not impressive. Even though international law no doubt plays a very important role in signalling the boundaries of legitimate activities, and serves as a key reference point in contracts and codes of conduct, it rarely plays a major role in actual regulatory efforts. Contractors are rarely held accountable at all. If they are, it is usually under various forms of national law and the few that have been tried for any wrongdoings are those convicted of economic crimes, such as tax-evasion and fraud.[7] This overall trend may be changing with trials involving Abu Ghraib interrogators, Blackwater contractors and the coup makers of Equatorial Guinea which all involve charges directly related to the use of force. But the outcomes of these trials are open and international law plays a limited role. Generally this is attributed to the technical difficulties

---

7 As detailed by the recent report Human Rights First (2008), this is not because there is a shortage of other crimes.

of using the hypothetically relevant instruments. However, a more convincing explanation is that there is a lack of political consensus around the adequacy of regulating PMSCs through international law and around what the aim of international regulation should be. This point will be made in general terms and elaborated specifically with reference to the difficulty of using the international regulatory mechanisms of mercenary activity.

The diversity and complexity of PMSC activity often makes it technically difficult to regulate with the help of formal international legal instruments. The reason is that much of this activity falls outside the categories on which these legal instruments are based. Basic distinctions between public and private, civilian and combatant, peace and war or between national and international are difficult to apply in a straightforward fashion. For example, PMSCs often operate as private actors but at the service of states. This makes the boundary between the public and the private (corporate and/or individual) highly uncertain (Dorn & Levi, 2007b). Similarly, the proximity and presence of PMSCs as private agents 'on the battle field' blurs the distinction between civilian and combatant (Heaton, 2005; Zamparelli, 1999). Finally, the lack of a clear line between 'military' and 'security' aspects of PMSC activity makes the categories war and peace difficult to employ meaningfully (Olonisakin, 2000). The difficulties of easily placing PMSC activities in legal categories render regulation correspondingly uncertain. It makes questions of applicability and suitability of indirect instruments central. PMSC activities consequently have a tendency to fall between potential regulatory mechanisms even when attempts are made to stretch and bend categories and interpret them as widely as possible, in order to capture PMSC activity. This is all the more significant as the use and enforcement of the formal international regulation just cited depends on the due diligence of states; that is, on states' willingness to enforce international regulations (UCHL, 2005). Uncertainty and disagreement about categories is an easy technical/formal excuse for not doing so, which is often combined with an outright and publicly stated lack of political willingness.

Indeed, the enthusiasm for relying on international instruments to regulate PMSC activity is limited. This is partly because any such regulation runs into the perennial difficulty confronting attempts to control and regulate security at the international level. Most states prefer to have strict control over their own security and are generally unwilling to delegate control over the use of force to the international level and/or to share information about their own activities. Since some PMSCs activity is specifically intended to circumvent national and international rules, this argument has substantial relevance both in the context of developing and developed countries (Walker & Whyte, 2005; Musah, 2002). More than this, the unwillingness to rely on international instruments to regulate PMSC activity is reflective of the overall hesitation to regulate markets. Indeed, market construction, outsourcing and privatising have been declared policy aims across very different contexts. The attachment to this policy has traits of a 'new religion' (Minow, 2003) with missionary overtones as it has been pushed onto those hesitant in adopting it.[8] Massive failings on most accounts, including the economic, humanitarian and military, have been disregarded and/or explained away (Reno, 2004; Rasor & Bauman; 2007; Markusen, 2003). Many states have not been willing to interfere with markets (national or international). This has severely hampered the innovative use of existing international regulatory instruments, not to speak of the development of new instruments specifically designed to regulate PMSC activity.

These general arguments are well illustrated by the limited role played by the 1989 UN Convention on mercenarism in PMSC regulation. Technical difficulties hamper the use of the Convention for this purpose. The Convention's definition of 'mercenary'

---

8 Military assistance and Security Sector Reforms (SSR) support is increasingly channelled through private firms and the market. The model that is promoted in this way is clearly one where the market has a place. For example, 'the SSR process in Sierra Leone has concentrated on constructing a Western-style security structure: an externally-focused army, an unarmed constabulary, and a small, tightly controlled armed police component' (Abrahamsen & Williams, 2006b: 16). According to some, the development of PMSCs 'can be understood as merely one facet of a larger philosophical problem posed by the United States' apparent combination of both the power and the will to ignore international law in multifold circumstances' (Coleman, 2004: 1494).

is, for example, often argued to be difficult to work with. The reasons provided are numerous (and contradictory). The definition of mercenary used in the Convention is amongst other things said to be problematic because it covers persons, not corporations, and hence misses most relevant PMSC activity. The definition does not properly allow for a distinction between legal and legitimate PMSC activities and illegitimate ones. Moreover, it emphasises the individual gain motivation, which is both difficult to prove legally and irrelevant. It is based on the nationality of a person, a criterion that might be both misleading (as it can change rapidly) and irrelevant. Finally, the definition is restricted to situations of armed conflict and/or armed activity aimed at undermining states and thus excludes most relevant situations including those where soldiers for hire are used in 'peace' situations, by states against their own citizens and by individuals or firms for reasons other than de-stabilizing a state. In addition to these concerns with the definition of mercenarism, the Convention has also been criticised for other technical reasons, including its purported lack of clarity about criminalization, extradition procedures, enforcement mechanisms and monitoring procedures.

However, the weak political support for the 1989 UN Convention is no doubt the key reason for its limited role in regulating PMSC activity. States have not been interested in using it innovatively to regulate PMSCs and/or in reforming it to make it more suitable for that purpose. The technical issues just indicated are held up as a reason for this, as is its timing and tone. The Convention was conceived in response to concerns that arose during the de-colonization struggle and hence appears anachronistic to some observers (Milliard, 2003).[9] The most significant reason the Convention has not been used is that many states have simply not been interested in

---

9 '...sovereign equality, political independence, territorial integrity, and self-determination of peoples' are the key concerns in the convention. These concerns are not outdated. However, by the time the convention was passed, the emergence of PMSCs, the end of formal colonial aspirations and the emphasis on good governance and capacity building had radically transformed the concrete expression of these concerns (Clapham, 1996; Duffield, 2001).

regulating the sector, at least not at the international level through the UN Convention. Regulation has been seen as potentially hampering efficiency, imposing red tape and potentially undermining the competitiveness of firms in the industry.

The weakness of the political backing is visible in the history of the Convention. The Convention was adopted in 1989 by the UN General Assembly, but it took twelve years for it to enter into force in 2001, when Costa Rica became the twenty-second state party. Today thirty states have ratified the Convention. However, none of the UN permanent Security Council members have ratified it, nor have key states for PMSC activities such as South Africa, Israel, Colombia, Sweden, Denmark or El Salvador. Neither do the parties to the Convention seem to find it an important and/or useful instrument for regulating PMSCs. Angola, Congo-Brazzaville, the Congo, Nigeria, and Ukraine are all signatories that have permitted or benefited from mercenary trade (Frye, 2005: 2642). Tellingly, the working group on the use of mercenaries tried to obtain information from UN member states regarding their views on issues relevant to the Convention. Twenty-three replied, some only to express the view that 'mercenarism' did not exist in, or affect, their countries (UN, 2007: 5, 9). In so many words, most states found the convention by and large irrelevant and were not even willing to spare the time necessary to answer a request for information about their views.

The example of the 1989 UN Convention has illustrated the general point that the existence of indirect international regulatory instruments relevant to the activities of some PMSCs sometimes has not necessarily helped ensure effective international regulation. The complexity involved in regulating PMSC activities that often defy the basic assumptions of the regulatory instruments available is part of the explanation for this. But the lack of interest in using, transforming and developing regulatory instruments is at least as important. The consequence is that formal international regulation of PMSC plays a rather limited role. Informal international regulation, voluntary codes and standards, fares slightly better. It is, by definition, adopted, and sometimes developed, by the PMSCs themselves with the explicit intention of legitimizing activities. As such it is integrated into PMSC codes of conduct, less susceptible to rejection on technical grounds and hence something PMSCs can be required and expected to follow. There are obvious limitations to informal regulation in terms of scope, content, monitoring, enforcement, and actual regulatory impact on PMSC behaviour.

Disagreeing about indirect international regulation

This account of the limited practical leverage of indirect international regulatory instruments raises the general question of what scope there is for expanding and improving formal international regulation and the role of external actors in regulating PMSC activity. One way of answering this question is to look at the current constellation of international actors and try to guess what is most likely to happen. Clearly, the more restrictive attitude that the Obama administration takes towards the use of PMSCs, its weaker ties to the 'industry' (although this really is a matter of degree) as compared with the Bush administration, and the increasing media/public attention to PMSCs makes it a rather safe bet that more international regulation is forthcoming. The Montreux Document is probably just a foretaste of what is to come. But to get a sense of what this regulation will resemble, it is important to know what kind of views will be involved in developing it. Drawing on the discussions surrounding the 1989 UN Convention on the finance and use of mercenaries, the chapter concludes by outlining the three general answers that coexist and compete with each other (the positions are summarized in Table 2). I will draw on the discussions surrounding the 1989 Convention to introduce them:

The conservative view is that one should not attempt to change or expand existing indirect legal instruments independently of what one believes regulation should be for. The general rationale of the conservative view is that even if existing legal indirect international instruments have many limitations, they have the virtue of existing and of being in place. This is a virtue not to be underestimated. International legal instruments are never easy to install and agree upon. This is particularly true with regard to PMSC regulation as there are intense and fundamental disagreements about what the aim of regulation should be. The expansion of legal instruments is therefore largely a chimera, and tampering (or even criticising) existing legal instruments to 'improve them' may in fact be counterproductive. It may perversely undermine their legitimacy. Rather than improve and expand the role of international law and external actors in regulating PMSC accountability, it may end up undermining it. With regard to the 1989 UN Convention, this position translates into an argument underlining that the best way to enhance the relevance and standing of the Convention is to work with the Convention as it stands, without expanding its role either through legal practice or through reformulations and redefinitions. In fact, any such effort at reformulating and altering the Convention is likely to perpetuate both the idea that the Convention is of marginal contemporary significance and to reinforce the related difficulties of finding political backing for the Convention and actions based on it or referring to it. Exponents of this view have included the states that have been most active in backing the work of the working group attached to the convention, in particular Cuba and African states who see the problem of conventional mercenarism as a continuing key issue, some of the working group members and many international human rights lawyers.[10]

---

10 Although the position of the working group seems to be evolving as they are now launching work on a 'parallel track' for dealing with PMSCs, implicitly at least underscoring that they think the Convention is inadequate for the purpose (Nikitin, 2008).

Table 2: Views on the role of the 1989 convention

	Conservative	Market Accommodating	De-Commodifying
General Rationale	Promote the convention as is with the limited aim of using it against mercenarism classically understood.	Acknowledge the legitimate role of markets and establish regulation that sort legitimate firms from illegitimate ones	Reaffirm state control over the legitimate use force. Take military security services out of the market
Suggested Action	Increase number of parties (common to all)	Restrict mercenarism: distinguishing it from PMSC activity Promotion of PMSC codes of conduct Blacklists and information exchanges on contract breaches Increased dialogue with PMSC firms and Interest groups	Expand mercenarism: include corporations Registration and licensing systems for PMSCs State approval of contracts Strictly limited tasks Expand monitoring and enforcement mechanisms
Implications for PMSC activity	Largely irrelevant	Legitimizing Extension of activities	De-legitimizing Restriction of activities
Implications for Convention	Irrelevance	Possible increased adherence to Convention Regulation of PMSCs is moved to national, market and firm level	Possible increased adherence to Convention Convention draws boundaries around legitimate PMSC activity
Exponents		The PMSCs/ professional associations Zarate, Milliard	Frye, Coleman.

The second view is market accommodating. The general tenor here is that private military and security markets are legitimate and that this is insufficiently acknowledged in a large portion of international regulation. Consequently, regulation needs to be updated to present day politics to acknowledge and make room for the legitimate market activities of PMSCs. As regards the UN Convention, the market accommodating view logically leads to suggesting that the 'postcolonial myopia' reflected in the convention has to be overcome (Milliard, 2003). Instead, the Convention could be reformed to play a useful role in separating legitimate and illegitimate PMSCs. This would allow it to play a role in the development of more effectively regulated markets. Practical suggestions to this end include redefinitions of mercenarism that would exclude legitimate PMSC activity,[11] the development of codes of conduct that PMSCs could follow and corresponding blacklistings of erring ones. A general promise of the defenders of market accommodation is that all legal change and development should take place in dialogue with PMSCs and their interest groups to ensure the effectiveness of the measures. Carried to its logical conclusion, the consequence of this kind of measures would be to legitimize and extend PMSC activities that could take place in a more regulated environment.

Quite contrary to the market accommodating view, the de-commodifying one considers markets for military and security services as largely illegitimate, dangerous and reflecting a minority political position. 'The rise of the corporate mercenary has effectively resulted in a divergence between the letter and the spirit of international law' as one legal scholar emphasises (Coleman, 2004: 1506). The main ambition of regulation should therefore be to re-establish and confirm the consistency of spirit of international law.[12] The 1989

---

11 Former special rapporteur Ballesteros suggested such redefinition in (UN, 1997).

12 Coleman further argues that the 'employment of the modern mercenary can be understood as merely one facet of a larger philosophical problem posed by the United States' apparent combination of both the power and the will to ignore international law in multifold circumstances' (Coleman, 2004: 1449).

Convention could be used in this spirit to underscore the illegitimacy of markets and to decommodify (take out of the market) the use of force. Concretely this translates into suggestions that would expand the understanding of mercenarism so that it could be used to condemn the market activities of PMSCs. In addition to this, it logically goes together with measures that re-establish and confirm state control over the market, for example, by introducing licensing and registration systems. Hence, PMSCs and their staff are under state or international control by creating mechanisms by which states register/approve contracts and/or by strictly limiting the activities in which PMSCs may lawfully engage. This position delegitimates PMSC activity, at least when it is not tightly linked to states and integrated into state efforts.

These three contradictory views underscore that international regulatory instruments can be used for widely diverging purposes and in very different ways, with diametrically opposed consequences for PMSCs. The obvious implication is that the basic question about the aim of regulation is of essence.

Conclusion

The agreement about the importance of improved international regulation and altered role for external actors in the regulation of PMSCs has just been shown to be shallow. At the most immediate level it leaves open the substantive issue of whether this is supposed to mean that we need more regulation or if it means that we need less. However, there is quite a loud discussion about whether or not we have an international legal vacuum. The chapter has argued that we do not. More centrally, this chapter has argued that the focus on whether or not there are legal instruments and whether or not the technicalities of using them make it possible to regulate PMSCs, through international law, is harmful to the discussion. It distracts attention from the substantive issue, which is what regulation should be for. As the last section pointed out there are three main positions on this issue: a legal conservative, a market accommodating and a decommodifying. These positions produce radically different views on what kind of actions should be taken to improve international regulation and what it may mean for external actors to take a constructive role in the regulation of PMSCs.

The constant implicit and explicit restatement confirming that we need 'improved regulation' is extremely unhelpful. It glosses over these far reaching divergences. It has at least two regrettable consequences. The first is that results – beyond longwinded technical accounts – are likely to be scarce. The second is it that it effectively sustains the de-politicising illusion that regulatory issues are technical. It effectively reinforces those who already have the symbolic power to construct solutions that appear natural to others. This chapter underlines that there is no politically neutral way to improve international legal instruments or reinvent the role of external actors. There are contradictory positions. Far more to the point is that the question of what position ought to prevail should be an object of open political debate.[13] Harking back to the consensus about the need to improve regulation hampers that discussion. The baseline is that the best way to ensure that the regulatory context of the next Nisour incident is different (and there will be a next Nisour unless PMSCs are banned, which is highly unlikely) is to create awareness of the different positions on the role of markets for using force.

---

13 I have argued elsewhere that the expansionary nature of markets is sufficient reason to follow a 'decommodifying route' (e.g. Leander, 2007b; 2008). This point will not be repeated here.

CHAPTER 2

The Privatisation of Security and State Control of Force

Patterns, Challenges and Perceptions in the Case of Iraq

Joakim Berndtsson

Introduction

On 16 September 2007, employees of the American security company Blackwater were involved in a shooting incident in Nisour Square in central Baghdad. The incident reportedly resulted in the death of 17 Iraqi civilians and spurred a substantial debate in the US and internationally on the use of private security companies (PSCs) in armed conflicts and the problems of holding the companies and their personnel accountable for their actions under national and international laws. Following the incident, several formal US investigations were launched and litigations were filed against the company. Blackwater were faulted by the FBI for their actions during the incident, and the US Justice Department obtained indictments against five Blackwater guards in early December 2008. Yet in spite of ongoing investigations, the company's contract to protect US State Department personnel was renewed in April 2008 (BBC News, Sept. 19, 2007; *Washington Post*, Oct. 3, 5, 2007; *Der Spiegel*, 2007; Scahill, 2007; *New York Times*, Nov. 13, 2007 and Dec. 6, 2008; US State Department, April 4, 2008 and Sept. 16, 2008).

The Nisour Square incident is one expression of the privatisation of security, a process whereby private sector actors operating in a global market are hired to perform tasks traditionally associated with state actors such as the police or the military. While instances of security privatisation are found in most societies, focus has often been placed on the use of PSCs to provide military- and security-related services in conflict zones. Indeed, employment of PSCs in high-risk environments has flourished in recent years, particularly after the onset of the wars in Iraq and Afghanistan. In Iraq, between 20,000 and 48,000 people are estimated to be employed by PSCs supplying a wide range of services to coalition state agencies and private companies working on reconstruction projects (GAO, 2006). The large number of security contractors has led commentators to describe PSCs in Iraq as constituting the 'second largest member of the "coalition of the willing"' in what has been labelled the 'first privatized war' (Avant, 2005: 8; *The Economist*, March 29, 2003). The potential importance of Iraq was expressed well by Christopher Beese, Chief Administrative Officer of Armor Group, who said that the case can be seen as a 'defining moment for the security industry in its provision of support to armed forces and reconstruction in hazardous zones' (Interview, C. Beese, July 19, 2006). Although it is certainly too soon to make any final judgements about the importance of the Iraqi case, its potential as a 'defining moment' means that efforts to understand security privatisation in Iraq and the problems related to this practice are both urgent and important.

The privatisation of security spurs questions about the relationship between the state and the instruments and use of force, as well as the changing nature of armed conflict. As several commentators have observed, the increasing use of PSCs challenges images of the state as a monopolist of violence and related assumptions about the primacy of states in the provision of protection and the conduct of war (Mandel, 2002; Singer, 2003; Avant, 2005; Kinsey, 2006; Chesterman & Lehnardt, 2007). The hiring of private companies to provide services in war zones raises concerns about the divisions of responsibilities and authority between state and non-state actors. Moreover, the fact that PSCs perform tasks that are conventionally associated with the armed forces begs the question of how the instruments and use of force are organised and controlled under these circumstances, and how state and non-state actors relate to and cooperate with each other.

This chapter will explore linkages between the use of PSCs and emerging challenges to state control of force by investigating security privatisation in Iraq and by focusing on functional, political and social aspects of control. The chapter draws on several primary and secondary sources, including government reports and a series of semi-structured interviews with people in the security industry. The following section will develop the theoretical approach to security privatisation and state control of force. Next, the discussion will turn to the case of Iraq, where the intention is to identify changes and challenges to state control of force following the privatisation of security.

The privatisation of security and state control of force

Security privatisation has been understood as a practice that leads to the introduction of market mechanisms, such as profit-maximising and competition, into the structure and organisation of activities such as national security and policing (e.g. Bislev, 2004: 599; Avant, 2004). In the literature on the changing nature of war, the term privatisation has been used in a wider sense to designate the increasing presence and impact of a number of essentially non-state actors, including rebel forces, NGOs, international aid organisations, guerrillas, private companies and warlords (e.g. Møller, 2005: 12ff). In this broad perspective, privatisation is seen as an indication of a general 'de-statization' of war where non-state and transnational actors play increasingly important roles (Münkler, 2005: 16ff).

More specifically, privatisation signifies a process whereby something that has been, or been seen as, a public responsibility is transferred to the private sector (Lundqvist, 1988: 4ff, 12; Feigenbaum, *et al.* 1999: 1). The responsibility for services can fruitfully be divided into three areas: regulation, financing and production. This makes it possible to speak of different forms of privatisation, such as the withdrawal of public subsidies or financing for certain services, allowing public services to be produced by private entities, or leaving the regulation of a certain activity to the private sector (Lundqvist, 1988: 14ff). This view also allows for the study of privatisation patterns in different cases. The term is a useful description of the current phenomenon, although it also needs to be recognised as potentially misleading: there is often a discrepancy between the 'clear-cut analytical distinction between public and private' in theoretical models, and the mixes of public and private that commonly exist in the empirical world (Lundqvist, 1988: 15).

To link security privatisation to state control, some authors have drawn attention to civil-military relations (e.g. Singer, 2003: Ch. 12). A basic paradox of civil-military relations is the fact that the institution created to protect a polity (that is, the military) is given sufficient power to become a threat (Feaver, 2003: 4ff). Hence a key question is how to make the military an effective protector against threats while at the same time remaining obedient to its 'civilian masters' (Finer, 2006: 6). Essentially, the military should identify threats and suggest appropriate responses to mitigate them, but only civilians may set the limit for what is considered acceptable risk to society (Feaver, 1999). The idea of state/public control over the military is particularly important in democratic systems: 'control of the military by civilian officials elected by the people – is fundamental' because '[c]ivilian authority allows a nation to base its values, institutions and practices on the popular will rather than on the choices of military leaders' (Kohn, 1997: 141). Hence a central concern of civil-military relations is to limit and control the influence of the military in politics.

With the privatisation of security, the composition of the instruments of force changes, and with it the basis for state control (Singer, 2004: 7ff). It has been argued that the inclusion of PSCs into the civil-military equation can have both stabilising and destabilising effects on civil-military relations and state control of force (Singer, 2003: 197–205; Avant, 2005: 253ff). The outcome depends on several factors, such as the type of company, the nature of the contract (what the company is hired to do), the type of client (public or private, strong or weak state), and the context in which services are delivered (war, peace, post-conflict reconstruction). Also, results depend on the meaning ascribed to the term control. Simply put, control is about the ability of the state to monitor and enforce compliance with the rules that it sets up (Thomson, 1995: 223). Developing this thinking, Avant outlines three basic meanings of control, each related to central themes in civil-military relations: functional control, which is about the capabilities and effectiveness of the military; social control, which deals with the integration of the use of force with social norms and values such as democracy, international law and human rights; and political control, meaning the subjection of the use of force to political or civilian rule and decisions (Avant, 2005: 5ff, Ch. 2).

All three dimensions are related to the institutionalisation of force; that is, the formal and informal rules and constraints that apply to the use of force by state actors and private companies, as well as characteristics of enforcement mechanisms related to the activities of these actors (Thomson, 1995: 214, n.4; North, 1990; Ruggie, 1998: 54). In terms of political, and social control, this entails the screening, selection, monitoring and sanctioning of PSCs and their personnel, as well as the impact of security privatisation on the promotion of (and adherence to) norms and standards (Avant, 2005: 56). In addition, one may look at aspects of functional control such as military capacity, or what Percy has called the 'military control over the use of force on the battlefield' (Percy, 2006: 17). On the same level, it is fruitful to study the relationship between state and non-state actors to gain a better understanding of how and why challenges to state control occur and what role PSCs may play in this context. To probe these issues further, the following sections will turn attention to security privatisation and state control of force in the case of Iraq.

The privatisation of security in Iraq

The extent of security privatisation in Iraq is unparalleled in the post-Cold War period. PSCs supply state and non-state clients with a wide range of services, including logistics, maintenance of weapons systems, military and police training and security sector reform (SSR), risk assessment, intelligence services, interrogators, translators, static guards, bodyguards, and armed convoy escorts or close protection teams (Isenberg, 2004; Pelton, 2006; Kinsey, 2006: 98ff; Donald, 2006: 15). A number of the people working for PSCs in Iraq are armed – especially those who carry out what Singer has labelled 'tactical services'; that is, guarding key installations, individuals or convoys (Singer, 2004: 6). With a large number of civilian security personnel operating in the country, and as a result of the number of incidents involving PSCs and their employees, the case continues to attract considerable attention. Yet access to reliable data is still scarce and so conclusions based on the case should be drawn with caution. Nonetheless, Iraq is a good case for studying privatisation in different shapes and forms, as well for exploring its potential impact.

Recalling the threefold division of privatisation relating to the production, financing and regulation of services, a quick glance at the use of private companies in Iraq is enough to reveal that all three 'types' of privatisation are represented and, more importantly, they are mixed. Focusing on which clients the companies work for, two tentative patterns of privatisation can be identified. The first pattern is the large number of different military and security services that are produced by private companies but financed by state institutions in the US or the UK. Here, a number of companies provide security services under contracts with state agencies such as the UK Foreign and Commonwealth Office, the US State Department and the US Department of Defense. The second pattern is represented by the large number of private companies producing protective services for other companies or contractors in the reconstruction project. These services may be financed by private funds or indirectly by public funds. Here, a large number of private companies are contracted by reconstruction contractors who are largely responsible for their own security (GAO Report 2005; SIGIR, 2007; House Committee, February 2007).

In both patterns, the issue of regulation is the most complex. While certain aspects of private security are regulated on the national and/or international levels, other parts of the companies' operations, as well as the relationship between PSCs and the armed forces, remain unregulated, and many aspects of existing regulation are seen as ambiguous, impractical or out of touch with the realities of PSC activities (Percy, 2006; Kinsey, 2006; Isenberg, 2007; Leander, 2007). Although state regulation has increased over time, oversight and enforcement are lagging behind, partly because investigation and prosecution are difficult in any conflict zone, but possibly also because of a lack of interest in pursuing legal processes (Isenberg, 2007; GAO 2006, 2008). In addition, both the US and the UK have proved willing to rely on a certain amount of self-regulation by industry organisations such as the IPOA (International Peace Operations Association) and the BAPSC (British Association of Private Security Companies) (Kinsey, 2006; Bearpark & Schulz, 2007). In sum, the case displays instances of privatisation in terms of the production, financing and regulation of military- and security-related services. The suggested patterns are hard to delineate because they display a mix and a blurring of public and private which, together with the extent of privatisation in this case, suggest changes in, and challenges to, state control of force.

State control in the case of Iraq

> Will Prescott: Why can't we use, say, the Army to protect people like Bremer and the ambassadors instead of companies like Blackwater?
> Colin Powell: Yeah, because the Army is limited in size, it's only about 500,000 troops plus a couple of hundred thousand reservists, and they can only go so far. And, you have an army to take the battle to the enemy and not just to be bodyguards. And if you can get qualified contractors – many of them are ex-service, ex-secret service and have those skills – then why not do that, OK? (*The Oklahoma Daily*, Sept. 11, 2007)

From this excerpt, three functional arguments in support of privatisation can be discerned. First, since the army is limited in size, it is rational from a functional perspective to consider private options in order to gain access to certain services. Secondly, because the primary function of the army is to fight wars and not to be bodyguards to ambassadors, using private contractors to perform these functions is a way of letting the army focus on its principal mission. Thirdly and finally, that security contractors are qualified to effectively carry out the tasks of protecting civil servants is indicated, Powell argues, by the fact that many of them have been trained by US military or law-enforcement agencies.

To reiterate, functional control is about the capabilities of the military and its effectiveness in defending the state. Letting private companies produce, say, bodyguard services may give speedy access to functions that are perhaps not readily available within the armed forces, thus enhancing, at least in the short term, the capabilities of state institutions. However, it could also be argued that outsourcing drains the military of core competences, exemplified in Iraq by logisticians and military trainers (Singer, 2004: 15). The loss of military competence to the private sector is a challenge to functional control: when private companies attract personnel from the armed forces (e.g. with Special Forces training), important and expensive knowledge is lost and states looking to increase capabilities by hiring private companies may end up paying again for skills they originally produced and financed (Singer, 2004: 9,16; Avant, 2005: 65; also Isenberg, 2004: 26ff; Kinsey, 2006: 107). Closely related is the question of how privatisation influences military capabilities and operations on the ground, e.g. in terms of cooperation between military forces and non-state actors such as PSCs. Because PSCs in Iraq often operate outside the military chain of command, it has been argued that from the point of view of 'military control', the companies 'add another level of complexity to the military decision-making process' (Percy, 2006: 17). In turn, this may result in problems or friction at the operational level (Percy, 2006: 17; Singer, 2004: 8f).

Examples of such challenges are found in problems of communication between different actors in the theatre of operations. Asked to describe the exchange of information between companies and armed forces in Iraq in 2004/05, one PSC employee said that official channels did not work well or not at all, but also that there were possibilities of getting information via personal contacts or informal networks (Interview, Anonymous 01; cf. Donald, 2006: 33). As one PSC representative observes, problems of communication and cooperation were sometimes very serious, especially in the beginning:

> There were times in the early days when you got nothing. Absolutely nothing ... you know, even if people were in extraordinarily dangerous situations, and we had one or two instances which I as an ex-Army officer found very hard to cope with ... when the military didn't come to our aid at all (Interview, S. Falkner, May 30, 2007).

Also, there are potential problems with the exchange of information between PSCs. Isenberg suggests that companies 'have varying access to information, and as they are in competition for contracts, there is a resistance to sharing such information' (Isenberg, 2004: 21).

Certainly, measures have been taken to improve coordination and the flow of information about safe routes, threat levels, etc. One example of this is the RSSS (Reconstruction Security Support Services) contract. The contract includes PSD (Protective Security Detail) teams, static guards, reconstruction liaison teams and support to the so-called ROC (Reconstruction Operations Centre) system. The ROC system was launched in 2004 and aims to improve coordination and cooperation between different actors in the field by processing information and intelligence and making it available to contractors. The British firm Aegis was originally awarded the $293 million contract to get the ROC system running and their contract was renewed in late 2007 (Donald, 2006: 71f; Kinsey, 2006: 105f).

Through the ROC system, declassified information from the military and intelligence processed by Aegis personnel is made available to commercial reconstruction contractors (or their non-state security providers), who can then use the information to plan their activities. The ROC is made up of several regional HQs or hubs through which it is possible to request, for instance, medical evacuations or military Quick Reaction Force, and it provides the military with information on the movements of reconstruction contractors and PSCs (Donald, 2006: 72; Interview, D. Donald, May 29, 2007). The decision to outsource the task of coordinating PSC and contractor activities and to relay information can be seen as a way for the US administration to improve functional control; that is, to get something done which the administration could not or would not do on its own (Isenberg 2007: 86). In addition, the contracting of a PSC to provide intelligence analysts as well as PSD teams clearly indicates a willingness to use PSCs as 'security experts' by making them part of the process whereby threats are identified, understood, and acted upon (e.g. Abrahamsen & Williams, 2007; Leander, 2005, 2007; Avant, 2005: 128).

In spite of initiatives such as the ROC system, problems of communication and cooperation persist (e.g. GAO 2006, 2008). The reasons for such problems are many: differences in organisation between private companies and the military; competition among private companies, and negative perceptions of 'the other' on the part of public and private actors are but a few examples. From the point of view of the military, there are different views of PSCs and their employees (Singer, 2004: 15ff). A senior analyst at Aegis writes: 'At an individual level it is probably fair to say British Armed forces personnel view British PSC contractors with a degree of envy' (Donald, 2006: 33). This purported envy may be rooted in differences in salaries, standards of equipment or length of contracts. In Iraq, some view American contractors as 'the top of the food chain' while others view them as 'cowboys' or 'mercenaries' (Pelton, 2006: 219; Interview, S. Falkner, May 30, 2007; Interview, Anonymous 01). Conversely, PSC employees fresh from the armed forces may have negative attitudes towards the military and may be disinclined to cooperate because they want to 'pay back for having been treated badly in the military' (Interview, Anonymous 02). From their perspective, they 'went from being pushed around to … pop stars' (Ibid.). Ultimately, tensions between these groups may 'undermine the loyalty, initiative and fighting power of soldiers' and thus affect the state's functional control of force (Avant, 2005: 261).

At command level, perception is also ambivalent, 'with accusations of poaching personnel and irresponsible conduct vying with an appreciation of operators' professionalism and the assistance they can provide' (Donald, 2006: 33). Again, negative attitudes will have functional consequences: 'Some commanders in Iraq … have been happy to ask PSCs to act as force multipliers … Other commanders have refused to have anything to do with the sector at all, insisting that personnel under their command have no contact with them' (Donald 2006: 33). When the views of individual commanders shape the relationship between armed forces and PSCs, this indicates a potential source of friction. Of course, different perceptions are found on all levels and not only within the military.

Asked about the relationship between PSCs and state institutions in Britain, one company representative replied: 'The MOD instinctively thinks PSCs may be a bad idea. The armed forces and the MOD are the slowest to consider the advantages that the PSC industry might offer and have been the least flexible at policy level in dealing with the reality of PSCs' (Interview, C. Beese, July 2006). Another PSC representative suggests that the MOD are on 'a steep learning curve about PSCs' and that negative attitudes may be shifting (Interview, J. Holmes, May 15, 2007). This was not the case early in the conflict, however, and the situation then 'contrasted vividly with the American experience, where they'd been working very closely together for a number of years' (Ibid.). Differences between the view of PSCs in the UK and the US are to be expected since the US government has a long tradition of contracting out various functions of the military to the private sector, while in Britain PSCs are primarily working for other private sector clients (Donald, 2006: 8ff; Kinsey, 2006: 98ff).

Taken together, security privatisation indicates several problems linked to functional control. On the ground, one important set of potential problems flows from the fact that PSCs are business enterprises. This means that they compete with each other for contracts and that they owe their loyalty first and foremost to their client; something that could make cooperation between companies difficult. As one PSC employee expressed it: 'No-one would bring their client into harm's way to save operatives from another company – responsibility to the client comes first' (Interview, Anonymous 01). Effective cooperation between PSCs and armed forces would demand structured working relationships and clear chains of command. In the case of Iraq, communication and cooperation frequently appear to have been ad hoc and largely dependent on personal contacts. While this image of privatisation and functional control cannot claim to be comprehensive, it points to important changes and challenges. To complement the image, we turn to the issues of social and political control.

In Avant's study, social control of force is about the consistency of force with social values, culture and popular expectations. The focus is on the impact of privatisation on the match between force and values that are at least in principle endorsed by the international community, such as democracy, human rights and the laws of war – principles and values presumably internalised by the modern professional military (Avant, 2005: 42ff). Political control is linked to the question of who decides about the 'deployment of arms and services' and about the allegiance of force to political structures (Avant, 2005: 5f, 40ff). In the civil-military relations literature, political control of force means civilian democratic control over the military and the belief in, and adherence to, the principle of civil supremacy among military professionals (Avant, 2005: 41f; cf. Finer, 2006: 25ff). Privatisation changes political control by redistributing power over the use of force among individuals, organisations and state institutions (Avant, 2005: 42).

Turning back to social control, adherence to more or less institutionalised 'international values' such as the laws of war need not disappear as a result of privatisation. On the contrary, many companies hire ex-military personnel from crack regiments of Western militaries, whose presumed commitment to these values they bring with them to the private sector (Avant, 2005: 60f). As a result, strong states that contract with companies whose personnel stem from their own militaries do not necessarily have to worry about social control. Yet adherence to international values – even among highly trained professionals from Western militaries – cannot be taken for granted. In the case of Iraq, one clear example allegedly including both active duty military and the contracted interrogators from CACI and Titan Corp. is the abuse of prisoners at the Abu Ghraib prison (Isenberg, 2004, 2007).

Asked to describe the situation in Iraq in 2005, one employee said: 'my impression is that it is a Klondike that attracts all different types of people. You've got everything from people with an incredibly solid military education to fortune-seekers and mythomaniacs' (Interview, Anonymous 01; Pelton, 2006: 343). Far from every employee of a PSC in Iraq is a former member of the Special Forces. As Kinsey observes, some PSCs have 'resorted to employing bouncers and security guards, provoking concerns about the calibre of staff providing vital protection services' (Kinsey, 2006: 107). Other cases are cited by Singer: 'examples in Iraq range form one firm hiring an ex-British Army soldier who had earlier been jailed for having worked with Irish terrorists to another firm bringing in an [sic.] ex-

South African Apartheid soldiers, including one who had admitted to firebombing the houses of over 60 political activists back home' (Singer, 2004: 9). These observations are not representative of the industry but they indicate problems of social control on the part of state clients – especially as there is a lack of oversight and enforcement mechanisms to ensure compliance.

However, changes to social control are not necessarily seen as a problem by states; they may even be seen as an advantage. Avant suggests that in Iraq the US have intentionally chosen to contract 'cowboy' companies ready to take on 'dicey' tasks, and willing to 'act like soldiers, not businessmen' (Avant, 2005: 226–28). For states, turning to PSCs may be a way of easing the pressure on overstretched military or police forces but also a way of mitigating perceived threats 'by proxy', thus avoiding public scrutiny or other negative outcomes (e.g. the death of citizens/soldiers) associated with using the military (Mandel, 2002: 66; Avant, 2005: 4). While these choices make sense from a functional perspective, concerns arise about the norms that are supposed to circumscribe contractors' behaviour. A case in point is the conduct of Blackwater in Iraq. US official investigations and hearings indicate that Blackwater has been involved in 195 escalations of force/shooting incidents between 2005 and 2007, including the Nisour Square incident. Blackwater currently holds a large contract with the US State Department to protect its personnel in Iraq (House Committee, October 2007). The question is if the allegedly aggressive behaviour of the company is the result of a conscious trade-off between functional and social control on the part of the US. While no satisfactory answer can be provided here, one interviewee expressed it in the following way:

> Blackwater has come in for a lot of flak over the way that it conducts itself in Iraq. I think one has to bear in mind the principal contract, or certainly the most visible contract that it's got, protecting US State Department people, pretty much requires that they behave in that fashion. I'm not sure that any other firm doing that job would be able to do it any different. The reality is that the US State Department is not going to allow one of their people to go out to a meeting in a beaten up, old, Toyota, wearing a rag over his head, escorted by three blokes, maybe two of them or one of them Iraqi,

and one or two of the others being Westerners with big beards and heavy suntans. They're just not going to allow that (Interview, D. Donald, May 29, 2007).

If the behaviour by some PSCs in Iraq is seen as aggressive, this may contribute to the increasing targeting of public and private actors alike (Bjork & Jones, 2005). Thus, in the eyes of insurgents, if (particularly Western) PSCs are associated with coalition forces and thus as part of the threat, then not only will this put armed forces at risk, it will also contribute to increasing insecurity for PSCs and their clients. This essentially means that the companies need to be recognised as actors whose behaviour impacts on the nature and logic of the conflict. True, state clients can and do try to influence social control by choosing certain companies over others and by promoting certain behaviour (Avant, 2005: 68). However, in order to promote (what is seen as) good or desired behaviour, the state would also need thorough knowledge and oversight of that behaviour. In the case of Iraq, and especially during the early period of the conflict, such knowledge and oversight was in very short supply (e.g. GAO, 2005, 2006).

In addition, it is not clear that 'undesirable' behaviour on the part of PSCs has any substantial effects. That incidents such as Nisour Square reflect badly on the US mission is clear; at a DOD news briefing in October 2007, Secretary of Defense Robert Gates said that there had been instances where the behaviour of private security companies had worked 'at cross purposes to our larger mission in Iraq' (DOD News Briefing, Oct. 18, 2007). Asked if he thought that the US could accomplish its mission in Iraq without the security contractors, Gates replied: 'Well, we could, but it would require an enormous commitment of American troops to … assuring the security of our diplomats and civilians working in Baghdad and in the rest of Iraq as opposed to working [with] the security situation for Iraq more broadly' (DOD News Briefing, Oct. 18, 2007). Commenting on the renewal of Blackwater's contract in spite of ongoing investigations, Patrick F. Kennedy, the Under Secretary of State for Management, said: 'We cannot operate without private security firms in Iraq. If the contractors were removed, we would have to leave Iraq' (*Time Magazine*, May 26, 2008). The statement provides a clear indication of the dependence of the US on private security companies and the apparent precedence in this case of functional over social control.

Turing to the question of political control, it may be argued that on a general level, outsourcing 'reduces the range of consequential control mechanisms by removing direct state authority over the setup of violent institutions' (Avant, 2005: 59). The organisation of private companies includes the companies' vetting or screening of employees. The fact that these functions are performed by PSCs changes political control because the 'control over individuals authorized to use violence slips into the hands of a firm rather than being in the hands of the state' (Avant, 2005: 59). As indicated above, there have been problems with vetting and oversight in Iraq. Even though companies have tried to increase their control of prospective personnel, problems of people lying about their education/training or criminal record do exist (Interview, Anonymous 02; Isenberg, 2004: 46f). From the point of view of the state, this means that it has to some extent lost the ability to use screening and selection mechanisms to ensure that 'the right sort of agent' is being author-ised and contracted to use force (Feaver, 2003: 78).

However, even if the contracting agency does play a significant role in deciding who can work for the company under a specific contract, there are potential problems if requirements are not specific enough or not followed up on. One PSC representative phrased the problem in the following fashion:

> The original DOD contracts under the Coalition Provisional Auth-ority, the CPA, was that an individual, going over in a war zone, carrying a gun, had to have prior military or law enforcement expe-rience. The type and length of military experience was not specified. Although the individual applying may have met the basic contractual requirements this did not mean he was qualified to carry a gun as part of a PSD (Interview, L.V. Avsdale, May 10, 2007).

This is an example of the contracting agencies not specifying the qualifications or backgrounds of personnel being contracted to perform armed services in a conflict zone. Effectively, this meant that PSCs were left in charge of the selection process and of specifying selection criteria. Under these circumstances, state authorities had little or no direct control over persons hired by the companies.

On the same note, the lack of adequate oversight has been pointed out by several commentators. Singer, for instance, writes that while the number of contracts has increased, the number of contract officers has decreased (Singer, 2007: 11; see also, Isenberg, 2007; Dickinson, 2007; Elsea & Serafino, 2007). Without proper oversight, the ability of the state – in this case the US – to enforce rules and policies, and to identify misbehaviour and fraud, is seriously hampered. Why this lack of oversight and enforcement mechanisms? North provides a simple answer that explains this from a functional/economic perspective: enforcement is costly. It is costly to find out if a contract has been violated, more costly to measure the extent of the violation, and still more costly to apprehend and impose punishment on the violator (North, 1990: 58). This means that putting in place comprehensive oversight and enforcement mechanisms may decrease the relative (economic) gains of security privatisation.

Another instrument of political control of force is represented by the Rules of Engagement (ROE) that govern the use of force for members of the armed forces. According to Feaver, the ROE are important because they restrict military autonomy, proscribe certain behaviour and require that the military report up the chain of command and inform civilian principals about operations, thus indicating when the rules need to be changed. As such, the ROE are 'both a leash on the military and an information source for senior leaders, civilian and military' (Feaver, 2003: 77). Thus, as 'long as the military operators do not "pull" on the leash, the senior commanders know that the pace of the military operation is less than the bounds set by the rules' (Feaver, 2003: 77).

For PSCs working for the coalition in Iraq, there are Rules for the use of Force (RUF) rather than ROE (Isenberg, 2004: 42; Isenberg, 2007: 88ff). For example, Tim Spicer, Chief Executive of Aegis, has said that Aegis personnel working in Iraq are operating under US Centcom RUF. Moreover, Aegis has its own RUF/ROE that specifically outline the circumstances under which the use/threat of force can be escalated and how this should be done (Spicer, 2006). Yet it seems as if there is still some way to go before the RUF can be seen as an effective leash on PSCs. One apparent problem has to do with information and feedback. Although all incidents should be reported, many have gone unreported, especially outside Baghdad (Interview, Anonymous 02). Also, there seem to be some problems with the roles that have been envisaged for PSCs. Writing about an incident in Najaf in 2004, Pelton argues that while the Rules of Engagement 'allowed contractors to fire in defense of their lives, the formulators of those rules had not anticipated contractors being dropped into a situation where they would have to engage in hours of combat' (Pelton, 2006: 154).

While issues of social and political control are complex and do not yield simple explanations or judgements, it is clear that the privatisation of security changes state control in several ways. Part of the explanation is in the differences between private companies and state agents such as the military. One difference is in what Feaver calls 'organizational culture' (Feaver, 2003: 80). In the civil-military context, the armed forces are expected to be willing to be subordinate because of their 'cult of obedience', or the 'norm of civilian control' or 'principle of civil supremacy' that is inherent in the relationship between the (democratic state and the professional army. Yet PSCs differ from this image of the military; their relation to the state is based on business contracts rather than social contracts. In this perspective, it is unsurprising to find that privatisation brings about changes in state control and civil-military relations, although the extent and consequences of these changes need to be examined further.

Conclusion

The aim of this chapter has been to explore linkages between security privatisation in the context of armed conflict and state control of force. Drawing a three-dimensional concept of control based on civil-military relations thinking and viewing privatisation as comprising the production, financing and regulation of activities and services, it has been shown that the extensive use of private companies to perform security- and military-related services in Iraq brings substantial problems of state control of the instruments and use of force. The framework moves beyond simplistic interpretations of the concepts where privatisation means the replacement of the state by market actors, and where changes in state control are interpreted as the breakdown of the state monopoly of violence and thus a weakening of the state. In addition, it suggests several ways in which security privatisation in the case of Iraq can be understood as changing and challenging the functional, political and social control of force on the part of states such as the US.

Certainly, the analysis leaves much to be desired in terms of empirical data. In the case of Iraq, more research is clearly needed in order to draw anything but preliminary conclusions about the impact on state control. Yet the examples from the case indicate that privatisation brings about institutional change and problems of state control on different levels. For instance, it is clear that functional arguments often launched in favour of security privatisation – such as increased flexibility, access to certain expertise, cost effectiveness – appear decidedly less straightforward when analysed in relation to political and social aspects of state control. Partly, the changes and challenges associated with security privatisation are connected to the differences in organisation between private companies and public or state militaries. Also, they are the result of a lack of regulation, oversight and enforcement mechanisms. Taken together, security privatisation alters to some extent the composition of the instruments of force and protection by introducing an external, commercial actor. As in the case of Iraq, this may lead to problems for established modes of control and channels of communication and coordination, as well as a role for PSCs in shaping security structures and policies. In a civil-military relations context, security privatisation means the creation of new civil-PSC-military constellations, and thus a need to pay attention to relationships between states and companies (civil-PSC relations) as well as between militaries and companies (PSC-military relations) (cf. Leander, 2007: 50).

From a broader view, the privatisation of security in war suggests a need for a critical reassessment of the ways in which violent conflicts are analysed and understood. This chapter has pointed to some problems related to the mixing of (and blurring of lines between) private and public actors and areas of responsibility in the case of Iraq. A major point here is to carry analysis away from a simple division of public or private, allowing instead for a mix of private and public that is more representative of the realities of armed conflicts. Obviously, the chapter has only managed to scratch the surface of these issues, and it has clearly left many loose ends. However, it contributes a basic point of departure for discussing and developing the analysis of security privatisation in relation to the nature of armed conflict and in relation to state control of force.

CHAPTER 3

The EU's Intervention
in the Israeli-Palestinian Conflict

Michael Schulz

Introduction

This chapter attempts to evaluate the interventions by the European Union (EU) for conflict resolution in the Israeli-Palestinian conflict. The EU has increasingly become involved in the Israeli-Palestinian conflict since its initial engagement in 1971. While remaining a marginal political actor compared with the US, it is by far the most important economic player for both Israel and the Palestinian self-rule areas on the West Bank and the Gaza Strip. Despite close political linkages with the US, Israel's biggest trading partner is the EU. The weak Palestinian economy is heavily dependent on the EU. The framework of the European Neighbourhood Policy (ENP), which was initiated in early 2002, aimed to ensure that friendly associated neighbours would surround the new EU member states. The Barcelona process, which was launched in 1995, also aimed to support and push forward the peace process between Israel and the Palestinians, while at the same time nurturing closer relations with the Mediterranean neighbours (Tocci, 2005; Gomez, 2003). The EU was the main economic sponsor of the Oslo peace process in 1991–2000, providing more than half the total amount of aid to the Palestinians. Given its strong eco-

Acknowledgement. Besides the editors' important comments, special thanks also go to Magnus Jerneck, professor at Lund University, for his useful comments on this chapter presented at the bi-annual Peace and Conflict Research Conference in Lund, 1–2 October 2008.

nomic involvement, the obvious question is to what extent the EU influenced and enhanced conflict resolution in the Israeli-Palestinian conflict? Hence this chapter will evaluate the interventions and role played by the EU in the Israeli-Palestinian conflict. Particular attention will be given to the political visions, ambitions and strategies of the EU. Furthermore, on what interaction levels (top leader, middle-range, grassroots) have these interventions been directed? Have the EU actions contributed to strengthening peace-building efforts in the Israeli-Palestinian conflict?

Previous research

Most studies on the EU emphasise its weak role as a diplomatic actor in the Israeli-Palestinian conflict (see Tocci, 2007; Miller 2006; Dachs & Peters, 2005; Hollis, 2004; Kemp, 2003). As early as 1974, Henry Kissinger claimed that '[t]he Europeans will be unable to achieve anything in the Middle East in a million years' (quoted in Gomez, 2003: 123). Most analyses of the EU and its foreign policy underline that with the increased integration the EU has formed a more united and coherent foreign policy. The Common Foreign and Security Policy (CFSP) was agreed upon in 1993. Despite the argument that a united foreign policy strengthens the EU influence, most analysts would agree that 'a careful assessment of the European record during the 1990s demonstrates that Europe has been of little influence in the monitoring of the Arab-Israeli peace process and the management of the numerous crises that emerged and currently hinder the whole process.' (Aoun, 2003: 289)

The EU has claimed to play, at best, an economic role by supporting the peace process, and enlarging economic cooperation with the Mediterranean and Middle Eastern neighbours, via the ENP Action Plan, the Barcelona process, and so on. Still, what is common for most of these studies is that too much emphasis is placed on the elite levels, or the diplomatic arena. They tend to downplay, or even neglect, the importance of other levels of societies.

Few studies have actually differentiated between the direct and the indirect EU actions and their impact on the peace process. Analytically it is not enough to claim that due to the failures of Israelis and Palestinians to make peace, the EU is a weak actor without any impact on peace-building. In order to conduct a more systematic study, we need to conduct a more careful analysis of the direct and indirect actions taken by the EU and see what impact the EU has had on the Israeli-Palestinian conflict.

By the same token, we still have no peace agreement between the disputants. The claim that the EU could have done more is also valid for other actors, not least the US, which is considered to be the most influential and powerful external actor. Hence, we need to undertake a broader analysis in relation to what type of conflict resolution intervention the EU has made in the Israeli-Palestinian conflict. One must also add the question of where does peace stem from? Does the shift towards compromise and peace emanate from the top leaders, from civil society, from below or from the international external arena? One could argue that without pressure from below, from the masses and civil society, it is not likely that their leaders and/or the international community can implement peace (see Lederarch, 1997). The external players must therefore not solely work in the diplomatic arena, but must also build peace capacities at other societal levels. The EU has consistently worked to strengthen various agencies and actors at different levels of the Israeli-Palestinian conflict. What impact have these activities had for conflict resolution between the conflicting parties? Also, to what extent can the EU be accused of having contributed to the failures of the peace process?

Model of analysis

It is common to assess the impact of a particular actor on conflict resolution by emphasising the diplomatic capacity at the top level. However, in this analysis other societal levels will also be considered. Moreover, the uneasy relationship between crisis management and long-term peace-building (or between security and development) needs to be addressed. One can argue that depicting conflict resolution as a process in stages; that is, prevention, peace-keeping, peace-making and post-war peace-building (Miall *et al.*, 1999: 16) hides the important role that peace-building and reconstruction may play prior to the post-conflict stage. Consequently, this chapter highlights the intervention by the EU in peace-building and reconstruction during an ongoing peace process, which includes issues of both dispute and cooperation between the parties. It also highlights the link between intervention projects and reconstruction and the improvement of life at a local level, as well as processes which take place among and between leaders.

Intervention is here broadly defined as 'a particular action, political, economic, military, with the purpose of affecting the management of a civil or international conflict, be it physically or structurally violent, carried out by a third party, be it an individual person, a non-governmental organisation (NGO), a state, a regional organisation or the United Nations' (Tavares & Schulz, 2006: 236).

Following the implications of the above definition, we can see a whole range of third-party intervention in conflicts. Post-conflict reconstruction[1] poses great analytical and methodological problems to development actors (governments, donor agencies, NGOs, the UN system), while it has been given relatively modest attention in academia. Peace and international relations researchers have traditionally focused mostly on top leaders, in relation to the pre-negotiation and negotiation phases of peace processes (Walters, 2002). However, in recent years processes at grassroots level and the post-violence phase have gained more attention (Orjuela, 2008; Goodhand, 2006; Reychler & Paffenholz, 2001).

Research on third-party involvement in violent conflicts is vast. However, few studies systematically include the different tracks and approaches a third party may use.[2] For the purpose of this analysis, Lederach's (1997: 39) pyramid societal model with the three overarching levels of entry for a third party will be used. One can

---

1 Post-conflict is commonly used, but as Forman & Patrick (2000: 13) rightly underline, the label 'may be misleading when applied to countries where formerly warring parties have signed peace agreements. In the first place, the conflicts of power, interest, or identity that spawn civil violence do not disappear after the cessation of formal hostilities. Instead, the parties to peace accords simply consent to resolve their difference in a non-violent manner through new procedures and institutions that may possess fragile legitimacy.'

2 For an overview of different tracks that can be used in peace-building, see Diaond & McDonald, 1996.

further divide third-party actions into direct and indirect interventions. This gives us six different overarching options for a third party to intervene (see table 1 below). (1) The most common approach is the diplomatic, so-called Track 1 method. Top leader politicians act as mediators and negotiate with the core parties in the conflict. (2) However, a third party may also choose to approach an agency that acts as a third party. This 'new' agency, for instance the UN or a single mediator, assumes the role of direct intervention on behalf of the original third-party actor. (3) The approach applied at the intermediate level is about direct interventions towards different Track II actors, such as 'think-tanks', civil society organisations, influential religious and local leaders, etc. The idea is to build peace capacities, which can pressure the elite to work for peace from below. (4) This may also be done indirectly by approaching the intermediate level of the third parties that in turn networks with the conflicting parties' Track II agencies. (5) Similarly, a third party may choose to support the grassroots levels, such as social movements, peace movements, local workshops, etc. (6) This can also be done indirectly with the third party's own intermediate and grassroots agencies.

Table 1. Different intervention strategies for a third party

	Direct	Indirect
Top level	1. From military coercion to diplomatic mediation. Example: US and Nato coercion on Serbia in the 1999 Kosovo war; Norway's secret mediation that led to a ceasefire agreement between the Sri Lankan government and the Tamil Tigers LTTE in 2002.	2. Diplomatic relations with other third parties to the conflict. Example: Member states urged the UN to push Iraq out of Kuwait in 1990–91. Arab states asked King Hussein to mediate and persuade Saddam Hussein to leave Kuwait in 1990–91.

Intermediate level	3. Involved in facilitating various Track II initiatives. Example: Swedish Foreign Minister Sten Andersson facilitated several Track II initiatives between Israelis and Palestinians in the 80s.	4. Give resources to Track II agencies' initiatives with the conflict parties. Also give support to different reconstruction efforts. Example: The Swedish NGO 'Life And Peace Institute', was supported by the UN and Sweden, in order to let them build the 'peace from below' in Somalia 1992.
Grassroots level	5. Mobilising social movements, grassroots organisations, media etc. Example: The EU in Eastern Congo directly supporting local communities, which aim to build peace from the local level.	6. Facilitating/ mobilising NGOs, social movements, etc. in order to establish networks with the conflicting parties. Also give support to different reconstruction efforts. Examples: Several European NGOs received support for starting grassroots reconciliation activities in Bosnia and Herzegovina.

Hence, it is an empirical question how the EU has acted, which approach has been selected, and how successful it has been in relation to conflict resolution in the Israeli-Palestinian conflict. Below follows an inventory of the chosen tracks and what impact they have actually had on conflict resolution. When reference is made to the collective actions of members of the EU, it includes the Council of Ministers, the EU special representative and the European Council. It is explicitly stated if the action is taken by a particular branch of the EU, such as the special representative, the European Commission (EC), or the European Parliament. The actions by individual EU member states will not be analysed in this chapter (apart from in the pre-EU historical sections).

Europe's colonial legacy in the Middle East

The historical record of the European actors in the Middle East is mostly linked to the colonial powers, particularly the activities of Great Britain and France. The competition between the European states and the Ottoman Empire, the intra-European rivalry resulting in the First World War, and the 'divide and rule' strategies, came to foster critical as well as hostile relations between Europe and the Middle East. The outcome of the First World War resulted in a division of the Middle East as well as the formation of new states in the region. Three agreements were signed between 1915 and 1917, which are still perceived by many Middle Easterners as the cause of many of the conflicts that erupted in the region, but which above all created a complicated relationship with many of the European countries. The first McMahon-Hussein agreement of 1915 was an agreement between the British and the Arab leader Hussein, who was the guardian of the holy cities of Mecca and Medina. In this agreement, Britain promised that the Arabs could establish a nation-state and in return the Arabs would revolt against the Ottoman Empire. The Syces-Picot agreement of 1916, signed in secret, between Britain and France, divided the Middle East into spheres of interest, along lines where many new Middle Eastern states were established after the war. This agreement contradicted the McMahon-Hussein agreement and when it became public created tremendous mistrust vis-à-vis the European powers. The Balfour declaration of 1917, in which Britain declared that Palestine was seen as a national home for the Jewish people, further contradicted the Arab objective of establishing an Arab nation-state.

These agreements, combined with a series of various actions taken by a range of individual European states both before and after the establishment of Israel in 1948, inflamed even more the already complicated relationship between Europe and the Middle East – not least, when Britain and France, jointly with Israel, attacked Egypt in the Suez War of 1956. Not until the end of the 1960s could a more coherent European voice be heard in relation to the Israeli-Palestinian conflict.

EC/EU becomes a new actor: 1970–1991

Since the Treaty of Rome and the formation of the European Coal and Steel Community in 1957, we have increasingly seen an integration process leading towards a more coherent European player. The European states made single-orientated actions in the Middle East until the end of the 1960s, when a more coordinated position gradually developed. Until then, one could see that France was more critical vis-à-vis Israel compared to West Germany, which had strong commitments to Israel as a Jewish state due to the Holocaust.[3] In fact, West Germany paid reparations for the Holocaust, which contributed substantially to the build-up of a modern Israeli welfare state during the 1950s. After the 1967 war, a more unified EC position gradually emerged. In the 1980s, the Venice declaration of the nine members in the EC stated:

> [T]he right to existence and to security of all States in the region, including Israel, and justice for all the peoples, which implies the recognition of the legitimate rights of the Palestinian people ... A just solution must finally be found to the Palestinian problem, which is not simply one of refugees. The Palestinian people, which is conscious of existing as such, must be placed in a position, by an appropriate process defined within the framework of the comprehensive peace settlement, to exercise fully its right to self-determination. (Dieckhoff, 2005: 53).

This principle has become a firm position, and particularly the Palestinians right to self-determination has been constantly emphasised, not least in the European Council meeting in Berlin 1999. Individual states came also to play an important role already in the pre-Venice period.

---

3 See further elaboration of this in Schulz, 1996.

For instance, the Swedish Prime Minister met, as the first Western leader, the PLO leader Yasir Arafat already in 1974 in Alger (Rabie, 1992). France became the first Western country to allow the opening of a Palestine Liberation Organization (PLO) office in 1975 (Dieckhoff, 2005). In 1988, Sweden was again instrumental in bringing the US closer to the PLO, which partly contributed to opening the road for the first peace conference held in Madrid 1991, marking the beginning of the 'Oslo process'. Below follows an elaboration of what visions, ambitions and strategies the EU has held since it formally became a European Union in 1993 by virtue of the Maastricht Treaty.

EU interventions: A multi-level approach

The EU has since the 1990s placed much emphasis on becoming a political player in the Israeli-Palestinian conflict. Yet the EU had to find alternative ways to becoming a player, or at least to be allowed to participate in the process, due to what Israel sees as a pro-Palestinian leaning as well as an American unwillingness to let the EU play a more significant political role (see Dachs & Peters, 2005; Dieckhoff, 2005),

EU's diplomatic capacity

The argument put forward in this chapter concerning the EU's diplomatic approach is that despite its sidelined role compared with the US, the EU played an important political and mediating role between Israeli and Palestinians, between Arab states and Israel, ultimately balancing the US influence.

At the Madrid conference in 1991, co-sponsored by the US and USSR, the EU was very much sidelined and marginalised. In practice, the process became an American 'high politics' affair in the different bilateral tracks,[4] whereas the EU was only allowed to participate

---

4 The bilateral tracks at Madrid consisted of one Israeli-Lebanese, one Israeli-Syrian, and one Israeli-Jordanian. The Palestinian representatives were included in the Jordanian delegation, however, and in practice an Israeli-Palestinian track soon evolved as well.

in the multi-lateral track (dealing with economics, environment, refugees, arms control and water). The idea was to let the EU spur regional integration ideas among the Middle Eastern parties.

When Israel and the PLO signed the Norwegian-brokered Declaration of Principle (DOP) in September 1993, the EU immediately came to the fore as an economic provider for the Palestinian Authority (PA) that was established in July 1994 in the Gaza Strip and the city of Jericho on the West Bank. More than 50% of the assistance by the international community came from the EU, with grants and loans up to 3.47 billion euros during the period of 1994–2001 (Dieckhoff, 2005: 55).

During the entire Oslo peace process, the EU made several attempts to play a more important role as a mediator between the conflicting parties. The EU's special envoy, Miguel Moratinos, put pressure on the Israeli government under Benyamin Nethanyahu. The idea was to improve Palestinian access to external markets, unblocking the Israeli restriction on free movement, as well as promoting new border-based industrial projects. (Gomez, 2003: 138)

Similarly, the EU attempted to pressure Israel to halt its efforts to build new settlements in the Jabal Abu Ghneim/Har Homa area outside Jerusalem, which was in line with a strategy to find a new diplomatic initiative by the EU. However, the EU could not bring Israel to change its policy, since Israel enjoyed US backing for its position. The EU role became more that of an actor that underlined the need to go along with a two-state solution based on UN Security Council resolutions 242 and 338. In fact, not until 2001 did an American president announce support for the idea of a two-state solution, and only in 2002 did the UN Security Council accept this formula. Hence the EU could be seen as taking a pre-diplomatic role, thereby preparing the political ground which the US and the parties were able to accept only later in the process. In short, the EU, despite its low-profile role, has had an important role in the long run in the conflict resolution developments.

In accordance with previous positions from the 1980s, the EU became in 2002 one of the four, along with Russia, the UN and the US, to propose the so-called Road Map for peace, suggesting a sequenced time schedule for implementing a two-state solution.

This is still the formal proposal that the American administration supports as the basic platform, and also from which the Annapolis negotiations began at the end of 2007.

Again, the EU could be seen as serving to balance the American position vis-à-vis the parties. Its economic ties with the parties, as well as with many other players in the Middle East region, can in the long run serve the EU. However, despite the ambition to create a greater momentum via the 1995 Barcelona process, and the various Mediterranean Partnership strategies, the soured political relations between Israelis and Palestinians clearly showed how these initiatives came to a halt. Hence the EU has, so far, not played a successful diplomatic political role that can shift the positions of the parties towards a more viable peace process. So far, the US has much more space for manoeuvre in relation to both Israelis and Palestinians.

The current stalemate between the Hamas and the Fatah movements in the Palestinian Authorities has also created a difficult diplomatic situation. The EU boycott against Hamas, in which Hamas has since 2003 been considered a terrorist organisation, has left the EU with few possibilities to act. With Hamas election victory, the EU could have played an important role between the Israel/US positions. In line with Israel and the US, the EU requested that Hamas should recognise Israel's right to exist, renounce all use of violence against Israel, as well as accept the previous agreements of the PLO/PA and Israel. Without downplaying the responsibility of Hamas' slow political, and often contradicting vocal actions during the spring of 2006, one can argue that several attempts to approach these requests were made, but were not acceptable to the EU (see Tamimi, 2007; Gunning, 2007). Further, the EU missed an opportunity to play a mediating role between Hamas and Israel/US positions, after Fatah and Hamas signed the 'Mecca Agreement' (2006). In this agreement, the parties stipulated the division of power and government seats between Fatah, Hamas and other political factions. However, Hamas declared its readiness to respect the previous agreements between the PLO/PA and Israel. De facto, a ceasefire was kept by Hamas after 2005, and it was ready to prolong this ceasefire for several years ahead. Furthermore, in its documents from 2005, Hamas had the intention of joining the PLO itself, which indicates a readiness to accept the two-state formula (Schulz, 2007; Hroub, 2006). The EU could have served as a mediating intervener, bringing Hamas into the political negotiations, thereby, creating a more viable potential for peace. Only Norway, a European country outside the EU, tried to take a mediating role, but did not succeed due to its lesser political influence.

EU's engagement with the civil society

On a general level, NGO activities in peace-building could be one influential factor in preparing public readiness for peace. In the 1990s and early 2000s, the belief in the importance of NGOs in peace processes was widespread and the donor community has been keen to support civil societies in the Palestinian-Israeli conflict. Hence, several donors became deeply involved in NGO activities, in particular with Palestinian NGOs. This also provided the EU with an opportunity to become closely involved with the conflict and therefore become one of the most important donors for the majority of the Palestinian NGOs. Moreover, the EU invested in various direct and indirect Track II and III activities.

One could argue that the EU worked within three different periods of the Israeli-Palestinian conflict, which differed in pattern, scope and content. These differences have consequently implied challenges for the NGOs, but also for the approach by the EU to address the relevant players and solve the logistical and security problems on the ground. Basically, one could divide the years 1987 to 2008 into three overarching periods: (1) the first *intifada* 1987–1993; (b) the Oslo peace process 1993 – 2000; (c) the second *intifada* 2000 – 2008. One of the similarities of all three periods has been the political goal of achieving 'normalization' between Israelis and Palestinians. In Israeli society, the establishment of 'normal relations' with the Palestinians has been a cornerstone for future peace-building. On the Palestinian side, however, a more critical viewpoint can be identified. One position in Palestinian society maintains that relations with the occupying power foster unequal asymmetrical relations and consequently strengthen Israeli superiority vis-à-vis the subordinated Palestinian side. Hence, not until Israel gives up all occupied land

and with the establishment of a Palestinian state can normal relations be built with Israelis. Particularly during periods of confrontations between Israelis and Palestinians, the issue of normalization becomes a 'taboo' question inside Palestinian society.

The EU has had a rather passive role in relation to the Palestinian NGO sector, but has vocally encouraged NGOs that systematically promoted an Israeli-Palestinian dialogue as a way to move the peace process forward. At the same time the EU preferred to have a low profile and could hence avoid becoming subject to criticism by hardliners on either side. Also, the EU avoided becoming engaged with the Hamas and Islamic Jihad civil society sectors since the EU did not know where to place the Islamic movements in terms of civil society. Despite the often taken-for-granted perception that Islam is incompatible with democracy and basically the counter-structure of a civil society, this is not necessarily the case here. The form of social infrastructure and networking established by Islamist organisations could themselves serve as a catalyst for more participatory politics. Islamic institution-building and networking in the form of schools, mosques, health clinics, kindergartens, charities, sports clubs, choirs, computer centres, etc., is a form of mobilization from below, although there are also instrumentalist reasons behind this. With these kinds of networks, a sort of parallel institution-building has taken place in Palestinian society. Instead of acting as an independent, autonomous sphere side by side with the state-in-the-making, the PA, Islamist institution-building aspired to establish a space in order to challenge the Arafat-led PA prior to the Palestinian elections in 2006, which Hamas won. However, the kind of social work and grass roots mobilization that is provided by this kind of organisation should be included in the perceptions of civil society. The EU's non-contact with the Islamist NGO sector has created a situation in which it becomes difficult to build peace from below – particularly so, since many EU-supported 'secular' donor-driven NGO organisations failed to meet the needs of the weakest sections of Palestinian society.

Many have argued that the first mass-based uprising, the *intifada*, breaking out in December 1987, implied a media breakthrough in the conflict. The coverage, including media from Europe, of the

Palestinian uprising implied a great political impact both on the domestic and international arenas. In Palestinian society, the first *intifada* was seen as support for the PLO, public resistance against the Israeli occupation and a struggle to gain Palestinian national recognition. There were no discussions on official levels. However, a number of Track II initiatives where launched. The *intifada* implied new self-esteem and political pride among the Palestinians. To the Israeli Labour party, the uprising proved the impossibility of continued occupation, and there was a growing sentiment in Israeli society that the status quo could not be maintained.

After the Iraq-Kuwait war in 1991, the first official negotiations between Israel and all its bordering Arab neighbours, including the Palestinians, took place at the Madrid conference. Many of the Palestinians who participated in these official talks, although as members of a joint Jordanian-Palestinian delegation, had previously engaged in civil society meetings between Israelis and Palestinians. Many of these meetings were held in various places in Europe. Hence the EU took the role as being a 'host' for Track II initiatives, but also initiated such attempts. Civil society, as well as individuals, began to discuss ways in which Israelis and Palestinians could meet and engage in discussions on future solutions. These unofficial (that is, associated people to the top leaders) or citizen diplomacy (that is, grassroots initiatives between conflicting parties) efforts were relatively few, but increasing in number. The purpose of these approaches was to increase the possibility of testing new ideas, as well as discussing the basis for the solution of some of the 'taboo' issues of the conflict.

The signing of the Declaration of Principle – the result of secret negotiations in Oslo-signified the starting point of a new era. The peace process implied a new role for civil society. A 'peace industry' mushroomed in which the EU played a major role. The Oslo peace process was seen, primarily by the donor community, as a post-conflict phase in which social reconstruction of Palestinian society and Israeli-Palestinian relations should be emphasised. Political interests of the international community in participating in the Israeli-Palestinian peace process basically invaded the area and the local NGO sector, particularly the Palestinian secular NGO sector.

Among other initiatives, people-to-people programmes were an attempt to strengthen cooperation between Israeli and Palestinian organisations through international aid. Also, think-tank constructs became replicated and the NGOs that were involved with the major conflicting issues (Jerusalem, Palestinian refugees, final status, Israeli settlement, etc.) produced similar output. In fact, donors developed a contributing role while the NGOs focused on fundraising strategies. Hence, little attention was paid to coordination between donors and NGOs. Identifying the real need as well as following up, evaluating and monitoring became a lower priority.

Many NGO activities came to an abrupt end with the eruption of the *al-Aqsa intifada* in September 2000. The collapse of NGO-initiatives for peace had to do with the impact of the overall conflict; the issue of normalization; the withdrawal of funding of many NGO activities; the inability of the donor communities to find ways to function in the conflict zones, as well as the unpreparedness of the NGOs to cope with the changes on the ground.

Atieh *et al* (2005) gave five reasons for the failure of the people-to-people programmes: (1) Programmes focused on the individual and did not affect the perceptions that participants held of the others' nation; (2) Programmes failed to reach important sections of society; (3) They ignored the socio-economic disparities between Israelis and Palestinians; (4) They placed too much focus on joint activities rather than inter-communal dialogue; and (5) The programmes implied an overly static view, with little reflection about the future or the painful past.

Supporting these arguments is the fact that many of these programmes were not based on a long-term interaction between the participants. Meetings of short duration and with limited space available for the airing of issues related to the past and the future are difficult to assess and evaluate in terms of long-term impact and sustainability.[5] Similarly, Abu Nimer found – in six different Israeli Jewish-Israeli Arab contact programmes – that 'for most participants this remained a "fun" experience that did not reach beyond

---

5 See Schulz, 2008 for an elaborated overview of Israeli-Palestinian conflict resolution encounters.

spending "good" time with friends' (Abu-Nimer, 1999: 127). The EU made an external evaluation of these activities and came to the conclusion that these programmes were inefficient and therefore should no longer be supported. However, due to the breakdown of peace initiatives – particularly in the Track I and Track II – paradoxically there was an even more acute need for citizen diplomacy and NGO initiatives than before. The withdrawal by the EU from these activities not only meant a missed opportunity to continue to build peace capacities with the civil society sectors, but also contributed to the collapse of important peace initiatives from below. The entire peace camp became paralysed, on both sides, as well as marginalised, making it thorny for the remaining NGOs that were working with peace issues.

The negative changes on the ground also had an impact on public opinion. So far (December 2008), the EU has not used or developed a public opinion-forming strategy vis-à-vis Israeli and Palestinian societies. The Israeli and Palestinian public have quite divergent opinions about the EU role in the conflict. Although occasionally they agree on the fact that the EU is a weak diplomatic player and could do more, it is always a judgement in relation to their own situation, and not to the overall situation. Hence Israelis have been increasingly worried about the EU barometers that show that Europeans are reluctant to see Israel's actions, such as extra-juridical killings of Islamist leaders (Hamas, Islamic Jihad), air strikes on positions in Gaza, or military incursions on the West Bank as justified. Particular concern came with the November Euro barometer (2003) that indicated that Europeans considered Israel to be the greatest threat to world peace. Europeans are seen as pro-Palestinian as well as pro-Arab in their position on the conflict.

The Palestinians regard the Europeans as weak, unwilling to challenge Israel and the US. They claim that the EU, with its strong economic ties with Israel, could do much better. Although they recognise that several single players within the EU are sympathetic, they are considered still too weak to make a difference. Because of the boycott against the democratically elected Hamas government, many Palestinians consider that the Europeans use double standards. Palestinians generally feel that the EU follows the USA and Israeli line, despite vocally supporting the Palestinian position. Public opinion polls conducted by the Palestinian Center for Policy and Survey Research (PSR)[6] indicate that most Palestinians consider that Hamas should bear most of the blame for the current stalemate between Hamas and Fatah. At the same time, Palestinians believe that external involvement in internal Palestinian affairs, primarily by the US, the EU and Israel, but also by Syria and Iran, is the principal reason for the current political turmoil.

Conclusion

There is still validity in the claim that the EU is a weak second-range player in the Israeli-Palestinian conflict, and this is in line with much previously conducted research (see Hollis, 2004; Tocci, 2007). In particular, support for this can be found when the focus is placed on the diplomatic arena. The US is still the most important actor vis-à-vis the Israelis and the Palestinians. However, it is also true that the EU has counterbalanced the American position, seen as pro-Israeli, by highlighting the needs of the Palestinians. The Israeli as well as Palestinian leaderships also accept the road map for peace, which is the political platform for how the EU, US, UN and the Russians are jointly working towards the implementation of a two-state solution. Hence the EU has played an important role, in balancing positions, as well as preparing the ground for a shift in positions, such as the Venice declaration of 1980 in which a two-state solution was declared long before US acceptance of this idea.

The more influential role the EU has played is linked to civil society and the grassroots levels in Israeli and Palestinian societies. The EU's massive support for the PA was aimed at building a democratic pre-state structure, thereby preparing the ground for a two-state agreement. Its willingness to support people-to-people programmes rested on the idea that peace should be built from below, thereby making it easier for the top leaders to compromise. Currently, the Israeli and Palestinian NGOs need to find ways to formulate a more sustainable multi-track strategy (diplomacy, civil society and citizen

---

6 www.pcpsr.org/survey/polls/2007

diplomacy/activities) both in short-term peacemaking initiatives, as well as in long-term peace-building efforts. However, the EU's potential to become a substantial contributor to developing a multi-track peace-building strategy was overshadowed by its need to be part of the game. This contributed to several flaws in their strategy towards civil society and the grassroots levels.

Firstly, the EU did not take a critical approach towards project implementation, which lacked proper auditing and economic reporting by the recipient organisations. Secondly, they forgot to approach the societal sector in which the Islamists acted, thereby contributing to their isolation. Thirdly, when the *al-Aqsa intifada* broke out, the EU chose to withdraw its people-to-people activities, simply because they did not work, without any critical assessment of why they did not work. Herein is a paradox, since it is more likely than ever before that people-to-people activities are required if a rapprochement between Israelis and Palestinians is going to take place.

In conclusion, the EU could play a very important role in the conflict developments by taking a diplomatic mediating role vis-à-vis Hamas, thereby working to shift the positions of Hamas and thereby bring them closer to the negotiation table. Finally, the EU could re-start a more cautious, but important, support for civil society, and the grassroots levels, in order to build long-term peace capacities that can impel peace from below. In comparison to the US, the EU is much better equipped for that role, and could thereby contribute to gradually building the much-needed willingness to compromise among both Israelis and Palestinians.

CHAPTER 4

The Changing Character of Peace Operations

The Use of Force at the Tactical Level

Kersti Larsdotter

Introduction

During the last decades, the character of peace operations[1] has changed in several ways. Before the end of the Cold War, peace operations were almost exclusively deployed in inter-state conflicts as a physical interposition between belligerent forces. The objective was mainly to create conditions for the parties to reach a political solution of the conflict. The military forces monitored compliance with the conditions of cease-fires and stabilised the situation on the ground, while the political negotiations went forward. Typical tasks were to control borders, to patrol front lines, buffer zones or demilitarised strips, and to supervise demilitarisation including disarmament and troop withdrawals (Bellamy *et al.*, 2004: 95–97; Doyle & Sambanis, 2006: 12; Pouligny, 2006: 1–2). Today, this

---

Acknowledgement. Parts of this chapter draw on the article: 'Exploring the Utility of Armed Force in Peace Operations: German and British Approaches in Northern Afghanistan' (Larsdotter, 2008).

1 Peace operations is an umbrella term for different kinds of operations, for example, peacekeeping, peacemaking, peace-building, peace-enforcement and humanitarian operations (e.g., in the US joint doctrine on Peace Operations (Joint Publication, 2007: 1–7), and the US army doctrine on Counterinsurgency (Field Manual, 2006: 1–20). For a discussion on different ways to categorise peace operations, see Bellamy *et al.*, 2004: 12–14).

kind of operation is often called traditional peacekeeping (Bellamy *et al.*, 2004).[2]

Since the end of the Cold War, the objective of peace operations is no longer to interpose between two belligerent forces, but rather to intervene in civil wars in order to create stable and democratic states. This kind of state-building includes economic reconstruction and institutional transformation, e.g. the reforming of the police, army and judicial system, the holding of elections and the rebuilding of civil society. Contemporary peace operations do not only aim at containing the conflict, but also address the root causes of the conflict, creating the fundamentals for a long-term solution. The first UN mission aimed at institution building in an independent state was the United Nations Observer Mission in El Salvador (ONUSAL) in 1991. These new ambitions have resulted in multidimensional, highly complex operations, including a huge range of tasks for the military forces, such as supervising and verifying cease-fires; coordinating the return of refugees; creating conditions for education and for information distribution; managing human rights and land tenure issues; ensuring protection of UN staff and equipment; creating security for the delivery of humanitarian aid, and creating safe havens for the population (Doyle & Sambanis, 2006: 14–16; Pouligny, 2006: 2–6). In this way, according to Béatrice Pouligny (2006: x-xi), contemporary peace operation forces restructure the domestic political and social orders, affecting the whole of society.

The changed character of peace operations has transformed the context of the military forces and the framework for the use of force at the tactical level of operations. While numerous facets of peace operations have been studied, such as ethical, legal and political aspects (Holzgrefe & Keohane, 2003; King, 1997: 13; Welsh, 2004), the actual conduct of forces in peace operations has received scarce attention. Nevertheless, several scholars and practitioners have argued that the conduct of military forces is of key importance to the outcome of peace operations. The robust approach of American

---

2 In this chapter, peace operations will be divided into 'traditional peacekeeping' and 'contemporary peace operations'.

forces in, for example, Afghanistan and Iraq is often criticised and compared to the softer approach by British forces (Thornton, 2004). However, there are surprisingly few systematic studies regarding the relationship between the conduct of forces and the outcome of peace operations, and the theoretical foundations are not sufficiently developed.

In order to enhance the possibilities of success in peace operations, the conduct of forces in peace operations will be more closely examined. The aim of the chapter is twofold. Since research on the conduct of military forces in peace operations is scarce, the first aim is to explore the theoretical foundations of the relationship between the conduct of forces and the outcome of peace operations by using theories of both peace operations and counterinsurgency. However, due to the changed context of peace operations, there are several challenges for the utility of force at the tactical level. The second aim of this chapter is to explore some of these challenges.

This chapter continues with a short description of the changing character of peace operations and why the tactical level of operations might be of importance for the outcome of these operations. In the following part, the theoretical foundations of the relationship between conduct of force and outcome of peace operations will be explored, and some examples from the International Security Assistance Force (ISAF) in Afghanistan will be used to illustrate the theoretical discussion. After that, some challenges for the theoretical assumptions on the utility of military conduct in peace operations will be discussed, and lastly some conclusions will be drawn.

The changing character of peace operations

In the autumn of 2001, a coalition of states, later under the name of Operation Enduring Freedom (OEF), launched an air campaign against the Taliban regime in Afghanistan. Shortly after, the International Security Assistance Force (ISAF) was established in Kabul and its surroundings. Today, the OEF mission consists of a counterinsurgency force of about 18 000 troops, mainly in the southern and eastern parts of the country, and since 2003 the ISAF mission has expanded throughout the country by the deployment of 'Provincial

Reconstruction Teams' (PRTs) (Jakobsen, 2005: 13; Lopez, 2007: 246; Maloney, 2005: 23; NATO, Expansion of NATO's presence in Afghanistan; Perito, 2005: 2–3). While the OEF mission was not directly authorised by the UN, the ISAF mission was authorised as a stabilisation force under Chapter VII by the UN Security Council in December 2001 (UN Security Council, 2001: 2).[3]

Today, the ISAF is an integral part of the International Community's comprehensive approach to Afghanistan, and its key military tasks include:

> assisting the Afghan government in extending its authority across the country, conducting stability and security operations in coordination with the Afghan national security forces; mentoring and supporting the Afghan national army; and supporting Afghan government programmes to disarm illegally armed groups (ISAF, International Security Assistance Force).

Furthermore, the ISAF contributes to reconstruction and development efforts by, for example, identifying needs, restoring infrastructure and supporting humanitarian assistance operations (ISAF, Reconstruction and Development). The multidimensional approach of the mission in Afghanistan makes it a good example of a contemporary peace operation.

This new kind of peace operation can be seen as a changed approach to the use of force, both at the strategic and the operational level. Traditional peacekeeping is founded on the notions of consent, impartiality and the non-use of force.[4] The notion of consent concerns the use of force at the strategic level, i.e. when to use force in global politics. Before the deployment of a traditional peacekeeping force, the consent of the main parties of the conflict has to be obtained; usually represented by the signing of an agreement, involving the commitment

---

3 OEF was launched as a response to the terrorist attack on the World Trade Center on September 11, 2001. The coalition launched their attack in accordance with Article 51, the right to self-defence, of the UN Charter (House of Commons, 2001).

4 The notion of the non-use of force is sometimes called the minimum use of force.

of the contending parties to a political process and their acceptance of the peace operation (United Nations, 2008: 31).

According to Alex J. Bellamy, Paul Williams and Stuart Griffin (2004: 2), the norm of consent is founded on a Westphalian notion of global politics; that is, on the notions of sovereignty and non-intervention. The role of peacekeepers is primarily considered to 'be limited to ensuring the peaceful settlement of disputes and orderly relations *between* states', and the domestic politics of states are perceived as of no concern of peace operations.

However, contemporary peace operations are sometimes deployed without the consent of the contending parties. This could be seen as a development in the approach to the use of force at the strategic level. According to Bellamy *et al.* (2004: 2), in a post-Westphalian notion of global politics, the domestic politics of states are considered to be closely intertwined with the international relations between states, and the domestic politics of states become the concern of international society. Failed states and substantial human rights abuses are seen as threats to international peace and security. Accordingly, the role of peace operations in a post-Westphalian notion of global politics concerns not only relations between states but also ensuring peace and security within states. At the same time, there seems to have been a change in the notion of sovereignty. According to Jennifer M. Welsh (2004: 2), the notion of sovereignty has changed 'from "sovereignty as authority" (control over territory) to "sovereignty as responsibility" (respect for a minimum standard of human rights)'. This change is reflected in UN resolutions. According to Welsh (2004: 5), most resolutions on UN interventions in the post-Cold War period refer to the 'transborder effects of humanitarian crises'.

The notions of the non-use of force and of impartiality concern the use of force at the operational level. The non-use of force concerns the norm of resorting to force only in cases of self-defence. This means that peace operations have been non-coercive, consent-based activities (Bellamy *et al.*, 2004: 95–96; Pouligny, 2006: 8). However, the norm of the non-use of force has changed to an acceptance of the use of force in defence of the mission (Findlay, 2002: 8; Pouligny, 2006: 8). In the case of the ISAF mission in Afghanistan, the mission was authorised to 'take all necessary measures to fulfil its mandate'

(United Nations Security Council, 2001: 2). This changed approach to the use of force at the operational level could be caused by the changed approach to the use of force at the strategic level. Since contemporary peace operations are sometimes deployed without consent, the level of violence in the area of operations might be much higher than in traditional peacekeeping operations, making the use of force in defence of the mission more important.

This changed approach to the use of force at the strategic and operational level might have made the use of force at the tactical level in peace operations more important. In traditional peacekeeping, where the containment and de-escalation of a conflict was of primary concern, it can be argued that the military forces did not interact with the society of the host state to the same extent as in contemporary peace operations. The contending parties in the conflict were of main concern, not the local population. The military forces primarily had contact with the armed forces of the belligerents, while civilian negotiators of the operation had contact with the civilian components of the contending parties (Findlay, 2002: 5; Pouligny, 2006: 44–45).

The ambition of state-building and the multidimensional nature of operations have made contemporary peace operations more entangled with the local society. According to Pouligny (2006: xi-xii): '[i]ntervening in a country through peace operations means getting involved, in one way or another, in a tangle of actions and reactions', and today most of the actors who interact directly with the missions are civilians. Furthermore, the changed approach to the use of force not only for self-defence but also for the protection of the mission has opened up for threats and use of force as a means of coercion at the tactical level of operations (Findlay, 2002: 6, 357). These developments might indicate that the conduct of forces could be increasingly important for the success of peace operations.

During the last decades, the approach to the use of force, both in global politics and in peace operations, seems to have changed. This might have made the use of force at the tactical level more important for the outcome of peace operations. In the next part of the chapter, theories on the conduct of forces will be explored, and some examples from the ISAF operation in Afghanistan will be used in order to illustrate the theoretical discussion.

The use of force at the tactical level

Apart from quantitative systematic studies with focus on the presence of military forces and on the number of forces deployed, force employment has mostly been ignored in Peace and Conflict Research as well as in International Relations (Biddle, 2006: 18). Research on the role of the armed forces at the operational and tactical level in these interventions is surprisingly modest, especially from a theoretical perspective. According to Robert E. Harkavy and Stephanie G. Neuman (2001: xi-xii), these levels have mostly been studied in military history, with a minor emphasis on theory, or as lessons learned by the military. The importance given to force employment is also evident in, for example, military doctrines and the training of military forces. However, assumptions on the impact of tactics and tactical behaviour on war outcomes are often implicit and, according to Stephen Biddle (2006: 17–19), nothing more than subjective assessments.

Nevertheless, as mentioned in the introduction to this chapter, several scholars, and practitioners alike, argue that the conduct of military forces is of key importance to the outcome of peace operations, especially the level of threat and use of force.[5] In assumptions on traditional peacekeeping, consent is thought of as crucial for success. However, it is only consent at the military strategic level that is of interest. It is argued that if the contending parties have consented to the operation and have signed an agreement, the operation will have better chances of success. This perception of consent presupposes a hierarchical structure of parties, where all levels of the parties agree with the political elites (Bellamy *et al.*, 2004: 95–96; Doyle & Sambanis, 2006: 14; Findlay, 2002: 4, 15).

In contemporary peace operations, the intervening forces are in close interaction with the local population. In these circumstances, it might not be the consent of the political elites of the main parties that is crucial for success. Charles Dobbie (1994: 124, 133) has

---

5 For those arguing for the use of minimum force, see: Bellamy & Williams, 2004: 2; Chin, 2007: 5–10; Jakobsen, 2005; Thornton, 2004: 83–84; Van der Kloet, 2006: 433. For those arguing for the use of show of force, see: Fearon & Laitin, 2004: 23; Mueller, 2000: 65.

developed the notion of consent. He argues that consent could be obtained at two levels, the military strategic level and the tactical level. Consent at the military strategic level concerns agreements between political elites, while consent at the tactical level concerns the will of the local population. Even if the operation has consent at the military strategic level, the intervening forces might have to struggle to get consent from the local population (See also Woodhouse, 1999: 30). This is also acknowledged in contemporary doctrines on peace operations (Joint Publication, 2007: I-2, I-10; United Nations, 2008: 32–33).

Unfortunately, the notion of local-level consent is not discussed to the same extent as consent at the military strategic level, and theories about consent at the tactical level are not adequately developed. Nevertheless, the notion of consent at this level in peace operations is strikingly similar to the notion of hearts and minds in doctrines and theories on counterinsurgency (COIN) (Hills, 2002: 2; NATO, 2001: 2–4 – 2–5). The perception of the local population is considered crucial for success (Joint Publication, 2008: I-5 – I6). According to the US doctrine on counterinsurgency, FM 3–24: '"Hearts" means persuading people that their best interests are served by COIN success. "Minds" means convincing them that the force can protect them and that resisting is pointless' (Field Manual, 2006: A-5). If there is a failure to win the hearts and minds of the population, the population might turn to the insurgents and the forces would lose the former's consent.

In order to achieve consent at the tactical level, or winning the hearts and minds of the local population, the use of *minimum* force seems to be essential. In doctrines on peace operations and counterinsurgency, the threat and use of force at the tactical level is primarily seen as a means of communication rather than a way to disarm the antagonists. For example, in 'non-combatant control', which is intended to influence non-combatant attitudes and behaviour in a manner useful to friendly-force objectives, it is argued that a balance between coercion and persuasion is needed. A combination of techniques could be used, intended to induce or coerce and expand or consolidate consent or cooperation. The threat of force is used as an instrument in both persuasion and coercion. At one end of the spectrum there are 'hearts and minds' operations, and at the other end 'search and destroy' operations: that is, a robust and forceful approach to non-combatants (Larsdotter, 2007: 213).[6]

With the norm of 'non-use of force' in traditional peacekeeping, the notion of minimum force is explicitly expressed. According to this norm, force can only be used in self-defence, and only as a last resort.[7] Otherwise, the forces might not be perceived as impartial and the consent of the parties will be lost (Thornton, 2000: 43). Minimum force is also emphasised in doctrines on contemporary peace operations and counterinsurgency. It is argued that the use of force might make the local population unfavourably disposed towards the peacekeeping forces, causing them to turn to the insurgents (Field Manual, 2006: 1–25; Joint Publication, 2007: I-5 – I-6; Joint Publication, 2008: III-9; NATO, 2001: 3–4). Although a show of force is sometimes seen as important for success in peace operations (Findlay, 2002: 356; NATO, 2001: 3–5), the use of minimum force is seen as the primary foundation of interaction with both the parties to the conflict and the local population. Their perceptions of the intervening forces are seen as important for the outcome of operations. By using too much force, or threat of force, the forces allegedly create or increase mistrust among the belligerent parties and the local population.

Peace operations include many different tasks at the tactical level where the threat of force could be exercised, for example when manning checkpoints, conducting patrols and escorts, collecting

---

6 In research on 'spoilers', as well as on terrorism, the threat and use of violence as a means of communication is prominent. Research on spoilers is one of the few areas where the impact of violence at the tactical and operational levels on peace processes is more closely examined. The use of violence by spoilers is seen as creating or increasing mistrust and decreasing the parties' willingness to continue the peace process (Höglund, 2004; Kydd & Walter, 2002; Stedman, 1997: 5).

7 Although the norm of self-defence has changed from 'defence of the peacekeeper's own person and those of his colleagues, using his own personal weapon' to include also the use of force to defend military posts, vehicles and equipment, force is still thought of as only to be used as a last resort (Findlay, 2002: 14–15, 355).

weapons, building schools and roads, and when meeting leaders on different levels. However, what constitutes the threat and use of force at the tactical level is not that thoroughly discussed. It could be argued that tasks not performed in public would not influence the perception of the local population to the same extent as tasks performed in interaction with the local population, thus making the *visible* conduct of forces important. In order to distinguish a more threatening kind of conduct, 'show of force', from a more friendly approach, 'minimum force'[8], certain features of the conduct of the forces could be considered. For example, the number of soldiers, the number and type of vehicles and weapons – as well as the kind of armour. A small numbers of forces, with non-protected vehicles and no visible weapons, are generally considered not to antagonize the population. More subtle forms of behaviour, like not wearing helmets or sunglasses, are also considered to have a positive effect on the outcome of peace operations (Chin, 2007: 9). In contrast, it could be argued that the use of a large number of soldiers, heavy weapons, many and well-protected vehicles, and visible body armour could frighten or agitate the population, making them turn against the military forces.

This distinction between different levels of threat of force at the tactical level is clearly noticeable in the conduct of forces in the British-led Provisional Reconstruction Team (PRT) of Mazar-e Sharif and the German-led PRT of Kunduz between 2003 and 2006,[9] despite a more or less similar operational environment.[10] Generally, both PRTs were involved in the same kind of tasks, such as escorts, meet-

---

8 In this article, minimum force is not the same as the British 'minimum necessary force'. Minimum force is rather about the *appearance* of the forces, than about how much violence they actually use.

9 Both PRTs were established in 2003 and the British PRT transferred the command of the PRT to Swedish forces in March 2006 (Jakobsen, 2005: 13; Swedish Armed Forces, Afghanistan). Hence the time frame between 2003 and 2006.

10 For example, the level of violence in the northern parts of Afghanistan is significantly lower than in the southern and eastern parts (Larsdotter, 2008; 365).

ings with local governors, chiefs of the police, and village elders, as well as advising and monitoring the Afghan National Army and the Afghan National Police, supervising disarmament, and attending official ceremonies. Long-range patrols were probably the kind of task where the military forces had the closest interaction with the local population, and where the threat and use of force, according to the theoretical assumptions above, would have had most influence on the success or failure of the operations.[11]

In comparison to the British PRT, the patrols of the German PRT were more numerous. Not only did PRT Kunduz have approximately three to four times more soldiers at the PRT, as well as fewer civilians in their area of operations (1 soldier per 23 000 civilians in the area of operations of the British PRT and 1 soldier per 4 000 civilians in the area of operations of the German PRT) (Central Statistics Office Afghanistan),[12] they also deployed more numerous patrols. Mostly, the British forces conducted patrols with six to seven soldiers, while the German forces deployed up to 20–30 soldiers on their patrols, displaying a much more robust force than the British soldiers. The PRTs also used different kinds of vehicles. When not in a hostile situation, the British PRT used unprotected vehicles, only two at a time. Outside the camp, German forces always used protected vehicles, often as many as 10 at a time. Protected vehicles, combined with larger patrols, could have been perceived by the population as a greater 'show of force'. In addition, the German soldiers always had to wear body armour and carry more weapons than the British soldiers. The British soldiers usually did not use body armour and they left the visible weapons in their vehicles when not in hostile situations.[13]

---

11 In the British PRT these patrols were called Military Observer Teams, and in the German PRT they were called mixed patrols (Jakobsen, 2005: 21–22; Larsdotter, 2008; United States Institute of Peace).

12 For a discussion on the number of forces vs. civilians, see Malkasian, 2008: 80.

13 For a more detailed study on the differences between the conduct of forces in the PRT of Mazar-e Sharif and the PRT of Kunduz, see Larsdotter, 2008.

Some challenges for the use of force in peace operations

Due to the close interaction between military forces and the local population in contemporary peace operations, it is argued that local consent, or the winning of the hearts and minds of the population, is important for success. Furthermore, local consent and the winning of hearts and minds are considered to be obtained mainly by the use of minimum force. Military forces in Afghanistan are conducting operations differently concerning the threat of force at the tactical level, despite more or less similar operational environments. These differences could make this level of operations interesting for further research. However, as a result of the changing character of peace operations and of changes in the context of global politics, the utility of force at the tactical level might not be as straightforward as suggested in the theoretical discussion above. In this section, three challenges to these theories will be explored.

The first challenge concerns the local dimensions of operations. It has been argued that military forces in peace operations are no longer interacting solely with the military forces of the contending parties, but also with the local population at large. However, in most theories on peace operations the local level is not adequately differentiated, especially not in relation to the conduct of the intervening forces (Pouligny, 2006: xi-xii). In doctrines on peace operations, the local population is distinguished from the parties to the conflict, but no further differentiation is made. Additionally, the use of force is considered to influence these groups in roughly the same way.

Some researchers have developed the notion of the local level in peace operations. Pouligny (2006: 45–95) argues that the local level could be divided into three groups: political, military and economic entrepreneurs; indigenous civil society; and 'local' employees in peace operations. The political space might not primarily be divided according to political groups, but rather along ethnic, tribal or generation-based lines. There might be shifting alliances between political and military actors and myriad economic entrepreneurs. Civil society might be composed of several groups; for example, informal organisations, community actors and religious actors. Furthermore, all these groups and ties are shifting over time. Andrea

Kathryn Talentino (2007: 155) divides the local level differently. She takes the primary focus of different groups as a starting point, such as political issues, access to power, personal wealth, economic concerns, justice, revenge, security etc. She comes up with five kinds of groups with different interests, and therefore different logics: elites, spoilers, citizens, victims and social groups.

Considering these aspects of the local level in peace operations, is it really credible that the use of force at the tactical level of operations could influence all groups in the area of operations in the same way? Even if only taking one kind of actors as an example, the complexity of the local level becomes obvious. In Afghanistan, warlords are argued to be important actors at the local level. According to Conrad Schetter, Rainer Glassner & Masood Karokhail, these warlords can be seen as, at one and the same time, political, military and economic entrepreneurs, and their loyalties are often distributed along the lines of families, tribes or clans. Furthermore, there are considerable differences between the systems of warlords in different parts of the country. In some parts there are a 'myriad of mini-fiefdoms, as well as localized "rules of law" or "rules of the gun"', where villages are ruled by ex-commanders from the civil war. In other parts, villages are dominated by tribal affiliation and in some parts the drug economy is of utmost importance for alliances between warlords (Schetter *et al.*, 2007). Making it even more complex, other aspects could be of importance for relationships at the local level; for example, different religious and ethnic affiliations, or the returning of refugees. It might not be surprising if people in a village affiliated with an ex-commander, living under the 'rule of the gun', would perceive the use of minimum force by the peace operation forces differently from people in a village with a warlord committed to the peace process. Or that people who were victimized during the Taliban regime have different perceptions of the conduct of the intervening forces than people who were part of that regime.

The second challenge concerns external 'audiences' to the use of force at the tactical level. Due to the increased globalization of media, the possibility for an international audience to be influenced by the use of force at the tactical level in a peace operation has increased. In his work on counterinsurgency, Ivan Arreguín-Toft (2007: 145–146) argues that there are five audiences for any policy or strategy in a counterinsurgency operation. Apart from the local-level audiences of the contending parties' armed forces, their respective supporting non-combatant population and political leadership, and 'neutrals', at the local level, Arreguín-Toft also includes the intervening forces military troops (friendly forces), their supporting populations and political leadership, and the 'neutrals' on the international level, as potential audiences.[14] The parties' armed forces, their respective supporting non-combatant populations and the 'neutrals' at the local level can be included in the local level of operations and have already been discussed above. However, the intervening forces, their supporting populations and political leadership and 'neutrals' at the international level, have not been addressed. For example, reports on different kinds of conduct of the military forces can sometimes create a great stir among the home audience, making them call for a withdrawal of their troops.[15]

Today, 61 states contribute to the ISAF operation in Afghanistan (NATO, ISAF Contributing Nations). Each of these contributing forces has a national audience at home to take into consideration. The use of force at the tactical level might influence different international audiences differently. For example, the use of tanks, a lot of weapons and many soldiers might seem reasonable to some international audiences but not to others. This could be problematic. According to Arreguín-Toft (2007: 146), 'any policy having a positive utility for one group or audience might have a negative utility for another.' If this is also the case for the use of force at the tactical level, differences in the use of force at this level of operations might not be important for the outcome of peace operations.

The third challenge concerns the multitude of actors in the area

---

14 I have adopted the different audiences according to a peace operation.

15 Some recent examples are, Lynndie England, posing with a dog-leash attached to a naked Iraqi prisoner in Abu Grahib (*The Independent*, 2005), Norwegian soldiers shooting dogs in Kosovo (*Aftenposten*, 2004), and the published photos of German soldiers desecrating a skull in Afghanistan in 2006 (*Der Spiegel* Online, 2006a; *Der Spiegel* Online, 2006b).

of operations. The multidimensional nature of contemporary peace operations has increased the number of actors in the area of operations. Furthermore, alongside the intervention, there are often a large number of Non Governmental Organizations (NGOs). In this context, does the conduct of military forces have any impact on the perceptions of the different audiences mentioned above? Or is the conduct of other actors more important?

The state-building efforts in Afghanistan are mainly coordinated through the 'Security Sector Reform' (SSR). Apart from the two different military missions of OEF and ISAF, a multitude of actors are included in the SSR. The SSR efforts consist of five pillars: the Disarmament, Demobilization, and Reintegration of Ex-combatants (led by Japan); the Military Reform (led by the United States); the Police Reform (led by Germany); the Judicial Reform (led by Italy); and the Counter-Narcotics (led by the United Kingdom) (Bonn International Center for Conversion). If just looking at one of these efforts, the Police Sector Reform, the German Police Project Office (GPPO), includes around 25 states and several international organisations in support of the reform of the Afghan National Police. Furthermore, the United States, which is the largest donor to this sector, channels its support, including contracted DynCorp personnel, through the Department of Defense's Central Command (CENTCOM). And, since 2007, the European Union (EU) and the European Commission (EC) are responsible for a European effort; the European Mission in Afghanistan (EUPOL). Apart from these efforts, several countries contribute economically to the police reform through the UNDP's Law and Order Trust Fund for Afghanistan (LOFTA) (Wilder, 2007: 18–28).

If looking at the civilian efforts of reconstruction and development, the United Nations Assistance Mission in Afghanistan (UNAMA) is the main coordinating body. Their objectives are to 'promote peace and stability in Afghanistan' and to coordinate not only all activities of the UN system in the country, and much of the coordination with the Afghan government, but also that of the different NGOs (United Nations Assistance Mission in Afghanistan, 2008). In the province of Balkh, only one of the four provinces in the area of operations of the British PRT of Mazar-e Sharif, 15 UN agencies and at least

45 international and national NGOs are engaged in reconstruction and development projects (Ministry of Rural Rehabilitation & Development). This can be compared to the presence of the PRT at Mazar-e Sharif, where only around 100 troops were deployed in 2006. According to Olson (2006: 1), there are more than 800 international and national NGOs in Afghanistan as a whole. The taken-for-granted assumption of the utility of the conduct of forces in these operations, seems less self-evident in this context.

These challenges present quite serious obstacles for existing theories on military conduct in peace operations. If taking different domestic and international audiences into consideration, existing theories on how the use of force at the tactical level influences the perception of different audiences need to be developed. Further research is needed on how these audiences differ from each other. For example, cultural differences in the approach to violence might be important (Larsdotter, 2007). Or different audiences' objectives might be essential for their perception of the conduct of peace operation forces. Furthermore, research on different kinds of media might be valuable, since media are considered important for the perception of international conflicts. However, if Arreguín-Toft is right about the problems of finding a strategy pleasing all audiences, it might be impossible to find out how to conduct peace operations successfully.

Concerning how the multitude of different actors in peace operations might influence the utility of force at the tactical level, some efforts have been made. 'Civil-military cooperation' has attracted some attention. However, this research is focused on how military forces can optimise their cooperation with civil organisations in the area of operations, rather than on how the conduct of different military and civilian actors is influencing the perception of different audiences. More research on the conduct of different actors in peace operations might be needed. The conduct of other actors in a peace operation might be more noticeable by the local population than differences in the level of threat of force by military forces. Perhaps the conduct of forces is influencing the outcome of operations only when the forces actually use high levels of force. In that case, theories and doctrines on the conduct of forces in peace operations need to be reconsidered.

Conclusion

Since the end of the Cold War, changing approaches to the use of force on both the strategic and the operational level can be discerned. However, systematic research on the use of force at the tactical level of operations is scarce and the theoretical foundations are not sufficiently developed. In order to get a better understanding of how to conduct peace operations, some theories on the conduct of forces in peace operations and counterinsurgency have been explored in this contribution, and some examples from the intervention in Afghanistan have been used. According to theory, the use of force at the tactical level influences the possibility of success in peace operations. It is argued that by using minimum force, the parties and the population will accept the peacekeeping forces and will cooperate. Differences in the threat of force at the tactical level at two PRTs in Afghanistan were distinguished; one that could be called 'minimum force' and one 'show of force'. These differences might indicate that the use of force at the tactical level in peace operations could be important for the outcome of these operations.

However, because of the changing character of peace operations, several challenges can be raised. The different audiences of the use of force at the tactical level need to be differentiated beyond the division between the belligerent parties and the local population, and both local and international audiences need to be taken into consideration. Different audiences might perceive the conduct of forces differently. One kind of conduct might be favoured by one audience, while, at the same time, it is despised by another. This makes the utility of force at the tactical level very difficult to explore. Furthermore, the huge number of both governmental and non-governmental organisations in a contemporary peace operation makes it questionable how much the differences in the use of force of the military contribution could influence the audiences, considering the conduct of other actors.

To understand better how to conduct peace operations successfully, and how to use force at the tactical level, further research is needed. The theoretical foundations need to be further elaborated and a closer interaction with other research areas might be a good way to begin.

CHAPTER 5

Witnessing the Unbearable

Alma Johansson and the
Massacres of the Armenians 1915

Maria Småberg

> In his mercy, God has given us, human beings, the ability to forget
> as well as to remember. We receive the grace of forgetting sufferings
> and times of anguish or at least the pain diminishes as time passes.
> How would many of us otherwise have the strength to live!
>
> Alma Johansson in *Ett folk i landsflykt* (1930)

Introduction

In 1915, the Swedish missionary Alma Johansson (1881–1974)
witnessed the Armenian genocide in the Turkish part of the Ottoman Empire.[1] Her accounts of the outrages are almost unbearable to
read. She worked in an Armenian orphanage in the town of Musch.
However, she was not able to save 'her' children from the persecutions. They were trapped and locked into a house, which was set on

---

Acknowledgement. Warm thanks to historian Eva Österberg and political
scientist Annica Kronsell, who read the article in an early version, and to historian Lina Sturfelt, who commented on it at a final stage. Their comments
have been most valuable.

1 Alma Johansson was sent out to work for the Female Missionary Workers
(Kvinnliga Missionsarbetare, KMA) among Armenian orphans in 1902. Later
on, she also worked as a midwife and after the genocide among Armenian
refugees until her retirement in 1941.

fire. Alma was devastated at not having been able to do anything for the children. She set out on a dangerous trip through a war-torn Turkey in order to reach Constantinople and give her report. Her testimony to American and German diplomats was soon published, together with the reports of other missionaries. After some years she published her story as a book.

In many ways Alma Johansson was a pioneer humanitarian professional, as she worked with helping civilians exposed to violence and with rebuilding a war-torn society. In her position as an external actor she became a witness to genocide. Still today, peacekeeping forces and humanitarian professionals witness crimes against humanity and are then forced to take on wider tasks and develop other skills than what they were primary sent out for. Through comparisons in time, a new sensibility for different scenarios and working on traumas can grow. The example of Alma Johansson contradicts the ideas of globalisation and humanitarian interventions as modern (post-1989) phenomena.

In this chapter I will specifically focus on Alma Johansson's perceptions and accounts of the Armenian genocide in 1915 and her role as witness. The genocide is considered the first genocide in modern time and an archetype that has influenced the perceptions of and encounters with later genocides[2]. It is also interesting to discuss Alma Johansson's testimonies with general witness literature in mind. The First World War is seen as the start of a 'witness culture'. However, the Armenian genocide did not constitute a central theme in this new genre, in contradiction to the place of the Holocaust in the witness literature from the Second World War.

At the centre is a woman acting in violent surroundings. In the witness literature of the First World War, the stories of the male

---

2 Genocide is generally defined as the intentional extermination of a specific ethnic, racial, or religious group. Compared with war crimes and crimes against humanity, genocide is generally regarded as the most offensive crime. Genocide attacks an individual's identity, and the object is control – or complete elimination – of a group of people. See the United Nations Convention on the Prevention and Punishment of the Crime of Genocide (1948). The Convention is built on the assumption that the Armenian genocide is the first example of a modern mass-killing.

soldiers are the most common. Here we find a female story, a story seldom told. The role of women in peacebuilding has also been neglected in research. In a period and region where women's freedom was limited, Alma took action on several levels. She challenged the ruling gender norms for women and war, but was also limited by them.

Within peace and conflict research, actors in civil society are increasingly in focus and their roles as advocates, mediators and peacebuilders are explored. NGOs and volunteer actions by individuals – for example, academics, culture workers, businessmen, sportsmen, religious leaders and women – are emphasised. In Alma Johansson we also find an early example of an external actor in civil society.

The Armenian issue

In 1915, between one and two million Armenians were killed in the Ottoman Empire. Persecutions and massacres of the Christian minority had already started at the end of the 19th century under the influence of extremist nationalism. The Armenian question is still a very burning question since the the EU demands that Turkey acknowledge the events as 'genocide'. Turkey refuses though, and the Turkish government also deny the high number of deaths. There are few eye-witnessaccounts kept. In this context, the testimonies of the foreign missionaries, such as Alma Johansson's, constitute unique documents well worth highlighting and closer study.

The Armenians claim a 3 000 year-old history. The people lived for a long time as a small Christian enclave in primarily Muslim surroundings. At the end of the 19th century the country was on the one hand a part of the Turkish region of the Ottoman Empire, on the other hand a part of Russia. In 1900 the Armenians were estimated to comprise 2 million of the 36 million inhabitants of the Ottoman Empire, while there lived approximately three million Armenians in Russia. When the Empire declined at the end of the 19th century, the regime looked for scapegoats. Stereotypes and prejudice about the Christian minorities developed and formed identity politics characterised by 'in- and out- groupthinking. The crisis led to the massacre of approximately 100 000 to 150 000 Armenians. When the First World War broke out, the Turks joined the German side. In the eastern part of Turkey, the Armenians decided to ally themselves with Christian Russia, the enemy of the Turks. They saw their chance to obtain self-determination (Gaunt, 2006; Gerner & Karlsson, 2005; Hultvall 1991). For the Turks this was an act of treason, and the government gave orders to kill or expel the Armenians. Most men were killed, while women and children were forced out on death-marches in the desert. These events are much discussed today, though. The official Turkish perspective holds that the persecutions were necessary since the Armenians constituted a large group of the population which had allied with the enemy. The Turks admit that in certain cases murders and outrages occurred, but there was no aim to exterminate the Armenian people. Some historians also claim that the issue of the massacres has been used as propaganda with the purpose of discrediting Turkey (for a discussion of this historiography, see Gerner & Karlsson, 2005: 123–27).

The most common opinion, which I share, is that the massacres constitute the first genocide of the 20th century and that it later became a model for the Nazis in Germany – apparently a people could be exterminated without reprisals. In 1915 the Allies promised international courts, but these promises were never implemented. After the end of the First World War, trials against 'Young Turkish'[3] leaders took place in Ottoman courts. According to the Swedish historians Klas-Göran Karlsson and Kristian Gerner (2005: 137–38), the courts in this period established that the massacres were the result of central orders, oral as well as written, and careful planning (see also Power 2002: 14–15).

Internationally, the Armenian issue was debated quite early, but it never reached the top of the international political agenda. It received serious attention in American and European media (Kennedy & Win-

---

3 'The Young Turks' was a common term for the reformist and nationalist political groups at work in Turkey at the end of the 19th century. Under the leadership of e.g. Enver Pascha, they came to power through a coup d'état in 1908–09. The Young Turks are seen as the initiators of the massacres against the Armenians (Gerner & Karlsson, 2005: 120–23, 135–38).

ter, 2004; Tate, 1998; Nassibian, 1984). Reports from eye-witnesses, chiefly foreign diplomats and missionaries, contributed to the attention. In the peace negotiations after the First World War, the question was not given much space, however (Gerner & Karlsson, 2005: 137, see also Moranian, 1992; Morgenthau, 1918; Toynbee, 1916). Alma Johansson also thought it was difficult to reach out to the wider society with her testimony. She wrote: 'After more than three weeks of tiring and trying travelling, I reached Constantinople. However, my accounts did not get much attention – the world was occupied with far "greater things", than the extermination of a small nation of three million people...' (Johansson, 1930: 44).

Nevertheless, influenced by the accounts of missionaries, Swedish activists raised the Armenian question in newspapers, parliament and at protest rallies. The Swedish theologian Erik Lindberg shows that the debate reflected national politics, as the right tended to defend the Turks and the left the Armenians. Hjalmar Branting, later Prime Minister of Sweden, participated in the debate and was among the first to use the term genocide.[4] In this way the testimonies of Alma Johansson indirectly reached wider circles, both in Sweden and internationally.

The Armenian issue was also essential for Alma Johansson's missionary organisation, Female Missionary Workers (KMA) (see Kurck in 'Tidevarv komma, tidevarv försvinna'. KMA Minnesskrift 1894–1934). KMA arranged funds for Armenian refugees; they sold Armenian needlework and arranged special days of prayer and informative campaigns within Sweden. Out in the field, Alma Johansson was working.

Witness writing

Apart from her accounts to diplomats, Alma Johansson wrote two books about her experiences of the genocide as well as on her work among Armenian refugees. She also contributed many articles each year to the missionary chronicle *När och Fjärran* in Sweden and detailed reports to her employer, KMA The first book was not

---

4 Hjalmar Branting used the term in a speech in Stockholm 1917 and at the League of Nations in 1920 (Lindberg, 1985: 264–76).

published until 1930, fifteen years after the events. However, parts of her story had come out before that in her reports and articles. In what ways were Alma Johansson's memories affected by these fifteen years? Was she, for example, influenced by other witness literature? To discuss the concept of 'testimony' seems necessary and fruitful. Traditionally, historians have been highly sceptical about this sort of material as an empirical source. Memory is often unreliable and it is difficult to view the history you live in yourself. On the other hand, witness writing can be used to trace the perceptions of people and their images of reality. We then must leave aside the question of what 'really' happened (Englund, 2001).

Within research on the Holocaust, videotaped interviews have been collected afterwards in order to be able to put people on trial or keep testimonies for the future. However, material from the old days, such as diaries and correspondence, has also been collected. This material differs in many respects. For example, Emanuel Ringel-baum wrote his diary to document what he saw in order to create source material/testimony for the future, while Anne Frank had another, more personal/existential aim with her diary. Both diaries are today used as 'testimonies' in research. For Alma Johansson, her outspoken aim was to make the genocide known to the public. However, I hold that her testimonies can also be interpreted as a working on trauma, which many scholars have shown was the case in a great part of the witness literature after the First World War (Tate, 1998; Herman, 1992).

The discussion of testimonies also links to research on witness litera-ture as a whole. The First World War had a big influence on modern witness literature, both as genre and phenomena (Winter *et al.*, 2000; Mosse, 1990; Hynes, 1990; Parfitt, 1988; Bergonzi, 1965). During the 1920s, numerous memoirs and memorial books were published, but also fiction, which dealt with the traumatic and horrible events that people had been through during the War (for example the novels by Remarque and Sassoon).[5] However, the Armenian genocide was

---

5 The historian Lina Sturfelt (2008) has written her doctoral thesis on Swed-ish images of war related to the First World War, especially in the popular press and novels.

not really a topic here (Tate, 1998). The question then arises as to whether Alma Johansson was influenced by this silence. Moreover, in the witness literature the memories of the soldiers are in focus. The British scholars of literature, Suzanne Raitt and Trudi Tate (1997), also analyse the writings of women in this context. Women had to handle a double role; on the one hand as active participants (for example as nurses), on the other hand as passive bystanders to the war of the male soldiers (as mourners of the dead) (see also Goldman, 1993; Hanley, 1991; Tylee, 1990). Alma Johansson also took on this double role, in spite of the fact that she was not a party in the conflict she lived in. As an outsider she tried by different means to save her dear ones, but her position was too weak and vulnerable. Instead, she was forced to see her children and colleagues sent to their deaths. She chose not to remain passive, though, but tried, in difficult circumstances, to at least report on what she had been through. Maybe her testimonies also became a factor bringing her a measure of relief?

The testimonies of Alma Johansson

In her witness writing, Alma Johansson gives an account of the hard time she spent barricaded in the German Protestant orphanage where she worked. In the orphanage other missionaries, children and Armenian colleagues and friends were also gathered. Intensive shooting had started in the town late at night, she writes. Groups of Armenians trying to escape had been discovered. The governor had told leading Armenians that within three days they would be sent away to Mesopotamia and all their belongings would be confiscated (Johansson 1930: 23).

From a window, Alma Johansson and her Norwegian colleague Bodil Biørn could watch how women and children were herded in the street by soldiers who shot at them to frighten them, laughed at them and hit them. As soon as one of them fell on the ground, a soldier came up with the gun-barrel. 'I will never forget this sight. And there was nothing I could do for them!' she writes in frustration. Many women took poison in order to escape falling into the hands of the Turks and to avoid being raped (Johansson, 1930: 24–25).

Eventually, the soldiers also came to the orphanage where she worked. Everybody in the orphanage, including the teachers and the pastor, must be extradited (Johansson, 1930: 28). When the time came for Alma Johansson to say good-bye to her children, she still had some hope of seeing them again. Concerning the men, they all knew their fate was to die. In this moment of meeting people waiting to be killed, her Christian faith becomes clear in her writing, and a wish to bring hope. To the children she says that 'nothing can take them from the hands of God' and to the men she says: 'we will soon meet again with the Lord.' (Johansson, 1930: 30). She then constructs a Christian image of how to meet difficulties with faith.

Later she heard that some Armenian men she knew had been led, bound together, to be shot at the city gate. Some women and children could be saved because Turks had declared them to be their wives, mothers and sisters. She was also told that 'the others, some hundred people, were either "buried alive" in great hollows outside town or locked into a house and burned to death'. This became too much for Alma Johansson and she could not bear to hear more. 'How I wished, those days, that a merciful bullet would hit me. Sometimes I found myself sitting in despair on the floor clutching my head, trying not to lose my mind.' (Johansson, 1930: 31–32). Later, some surviving girls confirmed the story that she had been told. Also officers and civil servants came to see her – with another purpose, though: 'It was obviously a pleasure for them to see me suffer from what they told me.' (Johansson, 1930: 34–37).

It is evident that the aim of Alma Johansson to report about the events to diplomats and in writing was a protest against the silence of the world. She writes: 'I will only write down some of my own experiences. Still, it is difficult to understand how the Turkish war of extermination against a whole people, could take place without protests, in front of the civilised world.' (Johansson, 1930: 7). However, it was difficult for the missionaries to reach out since everything they wrote became subject to censorship: 'We missionaries did not dare to write home and tell what was going on. The letters were strongly censored.' (Johansson, 1930: 14).

In the preface to Alma Johansson's *Ett folk i landsflykt*, the KMA worker Sigrid Kurck describes how Alma had returned to Sweden in 1915 with a face marked by pain and suffering: 'For a long time she could not speak about the most difficult, the fate of the little ones!' (Kurck in Johansson 1930: 4). It took time for her to recover. In 1920 she went out again, to work among Armenian refugees in Constantinople and soon also in Greece. Practical work became for her a way to work on the trauma and do something constructive, to move on. But her writings also served this end, I argue. As a survivor she was marked by living with agony, but also with guilt, which she needed to work on:

> When, at last, the thought imposed my mind, that I now had to count on life again, I was depressed. I needed time to settle down again in life. And for some years the thought of having to live on was almost unbearable to me. And still there were moments, when it feels so difficult that I was not among those who could follow the others home, but was left almost alone (Johansson, 1930: 44).

Behind the testimonies of Alma Johansson, we find a need to protest against the world's silence, but also to work on the trauma she has been through. In both cases she makes herself into an active subject. It can, of course, be discussed if she is exaggerating her role because of her feelings of guilt. We also find a contradiction here. Alma Johansson's accounts are important eye-witness source material; at the same time she is trying to leave history behind.

If we then look closer at her text, what perceptions do we find of Alma Johansson as an external actor and witness of genocide? In today's research, witnesses are not only seen as observers with first-hand information which can be used as testimony or documentation. William L. Ury at Harvard Law School shows how witnesses can also prevent violence through detecting early warning signals, going on patrol, speaking out and getting help fast (Ury, 2000).[6] In this close study, I want especially to focus on Alma's role as a female missionary and civil actor in a conflict situation in order to find out more about her wider tasks as a witness.

---

6 Ury describes how witnesses, by watching carefully, can help spot emerging ethnic conflicts before they break out into violence. However, witnesses can also be actively present in hotspots. They can speak out to persuade the parties to cease fighting or respect agreements. They can also call the attention of other interveners and the media.

Missionary from the the West

When Alma Johansson went out as a missionary in 1902, she did so without romantic dreams, according to herself:

> I had heard so much from my field of mission, especially during my stay at the missionary school, which made it impossible to have any romantic dreams. It was to 'the land of blood and tears' I had received my call .... But I prepared myself for all difficulties, hardships and sufferings, which could arrive. This became a great help for me and spared me from many disappointments (Johansson, 1944: 63).

She then describes how on arrival she had suffered from severe malaria fever and that the journey through Turkey had been 'more than just difficult'. When she finally arrived she could find nothing beautiful or interesting. 'But it was here I had found my task, and that filled me with joy', Alma Johansson writes, nevertheless. The meeting with the seven hundred children who had lost their parents in massacres filled her with eagerness to take care of some of them (Johansson, 1944: 63–64).

Alma Johansson and the other missionaries had direct contact with the local population, as they provided them with medical treatment in the polyclinic and by visiting the homes in the town and villages. She writes that she lived close to them and that she really learned to understand them: 'When they – one after the other – told me their story and about all discrimination they had been exposed to, I saw that they all shared the membership of an oppressed people, that "the sword" was part of their past, not only for one generation, but as long as they could remember.' Certainly, she claims that the injustice and suffering 'had distorted their concept of justice', but at the same time she found among them a love which she learned to 'respect and value' (Johansson, 1924: 29). In a way, Alma Johansson describes herself as an empathic listener[7].

---

7 Empathic listening (also called active listening or reflective listening) is a way of listening and responding to another person that improves mutual understanding and trust. It has been recognised as an essential skill for third parties in negotiation or mediation situations to resolve or transform community conflicts (Salem 1982).

On the other hand, in her texts Alma Johansson also expresses attitudes connected to Orientalism when she describes the people she meets in a stereotypical way.[8] During the years of war she met, for example, men in the street who shouted at her, blaming her for all troubles: 'And so they started to curse me with all the dirty words an Oriental possesses.' The 'Oriental', the 'Other', is pictured as someone who easily loses his temper and uses rough language. She describes herself as calm and how she listens until the group of men stopped and left her alone (Johansson, 1930: 20). In this way she becomes the opposite of the 'Oriental' – sensible and civilised.

Alma Johansson also describes a case when she was called upon to assist the sister of the governor, who was ill. However, Alma was very afraid: 'The husband of the sick [woman] was, in spite of his official status, an unusually rude, dirty and uneducated Moham-medan, including all what that word means.' She had to eat from the same plate as he and his friends and she found it very distasteful (Johansson, 1930: 16). The Muslims she is describing here are, in her eyes, obviously on a lower level in terms of civilisation.

She often returns to describing Turkish officials and soldiers as hot-tempered, aggressive and brutal (Johansson, 1930: 9–10, 12–14, 23–25). In a cruel episode, Alma Johansson tells how the governor met a group of Armenians who had been to the Caucasian front. The governor became very angry over a sick man and hit him with his riding-whip: 'I will show you that I feel no mercy', he said. Alma Johansson writes that the man was killed by the governor's whip (Johansson, 1930: 9–10). The image of the Turks as perpetrators becomes evident here.

The Armenians, on the other hand, are described as passive victims or people who meet difficulties and aggression with calmness, cour-age and nobility. After soldiers had plundered Armenian homes and shops, Alma writes that the Armenians kept calm: 'because they knew that any resistance from a single Armenian could mean the start of

---

8 Edward W. Said discusses how, for example, Western authors and scholars have spread stereotypical images of people in a fictive Orient. In this way, a dichotomy between East and West, us and them, was created. Thus, Oriental-ism also became a tool of power (Said, 1993, 1978).

a massacre' (Johansson, 1930: 12–14). One can, of course, discuss whether one can describe the Armenians as brave when keeping calm under such circumstances, or if they acted out of an instinct to survive. The official Turks, on the other hand, singled out the Armenians as rebellious, which legitimised the persecutions. Alma Johansson then creates a counter-narrative to the official Turkish-nationalistic version. She portrays men as passive victims of war in opposition to the traditional image of the war hero. Different images of masculinity emerge in this way. This is interesting from a gender perspective, something I will return to later on. Witness literature of the First World War partly created this change in the view of the war hero and victim (e.g. Sturfelt, 2008).

However, Alma does not judge every Turk or Muslim alike. In a final attempt to save the last women and children from death, she contacts a captain whose wife she had nursed, and she writes: 'He was a human being, although he was a Mohammedan, and I recognised that he was ashamed on behalf of his people. He immediately promised to visit the governor and demand the liberation of the young female teachers' (Johansson, 1930: 32). Her statement is Islamophobic, albeit at the same time showing how the Muslim can be benevolent. The Norwegian historian Inger Marie Okkenhaug, who has studied Alma Johansson's colleague Bodil Biørn, claims that when the Scandinavian Armenian missionaries portray the different ethnic groups they were in contact with, they give a more nuanced image of the multicultural and multi-religious Ottoman Empire than was usual among their contemporaries. The Muslims had different ethnic belonging: Turkish, Kurdish and Arab. Moreover, the missionaries point to the differences between various branches within Islam. In their contacts with the local Muslim population, the Muslims also become individualised, Okkenhaug (2006) stresses.[9] To me it is interesting to stress both tendencies; that there exist stereotypes and openness towards others simultaneously in the text. It creates a dynamic interplay between different positions and openness for the ambivalence of human nature.

---

9 See also Melman (1995), who argues that there exists an alternative female Orientalist discourse which is more multifaceted and complex.

When the Turkish nationalism flares up, the attitudes towards the Christian minorities in the region change radically towards identity politics. The Turks viewed the Christians more and more as enemies of the state. A religious frame of interpretation would therefore be an easy stand to take. As the image of the Muslims that Alma Johansson held spread to her Swedish audience, it becomes even more interesting to study. However, for her it is Turks, Kurds and Albanians who commit crimes, not 'the Muslim'. As the incident above indicates, she also describes how Turkish Muslims protected and helped Armenians. When she writes about 'Muslims' she is certainly referring to them as less civilised, but actually not as perpetrators.

Concerning her view of herself as a missionary, it deals more with helping and giving hope than about converting other people. In the depressing conditions under which the Armenians lived, they needed support in order not to lose their faith – not only spiritual help but also physical and moral (Johansson, 1930: 36, 1924: 30–31). The reason why Alma Johansson's intention was not to convert can partly be found in the fact that she mainly worked among a people who were already Christian. However, one could also expect that she had wanted them to become Christian in 'the right Protestant way'. The Danish historian Matthias Bjørnlund shows that when the Armenians had the choice to convert to Islam or die, Danish evangelical missionaries supported them in sacrificing their lives for their faith (Bjørnlund, 2005, 2006). This is nothing Alma Johansson advocates, but she writes that: '… all Armenians have certainly not had the direct choice to deny Christ, but most of them could have escaped these sufferings *if* they had chosen to become Mohammedans. But they were faithful to our Lord, a faithfulness that has gained its strength from the faithfulness of God.' (Johansson, 1930: 46). In retrospect, Alma Johansson comes to the conclusion that it was after all better to die for one's faith.

When Alma Johansson looks back at her work during the war and the many Armenian victims, she tries to find a meaning to the suffering. Here she focuses on the testimony about the genocide and earlier actions of assistance or acts of love:

We did not try to escape–we were forced to leave. Maybe the Lord wanted some witnesses to what had happened, because they are not willing to give credit to the Armenian testimonies. Now they are at home with God, all those among whom we have worked, prayed and hoped for and many times battled death for their lives. Was this the result of all the years of duty, of the prayers and sacrifices by the mission? Yes, in external appearance it looks demolished, and my heart is struck by a deep sadness. But we also know that what we have done out of love for the Lord can never have been in vain (Johansson, 1944: 66).

All the work had, after all, not been in vain. At the same time, she claims that God used the Turks to lead those Armenians to heaven who, during calmer circumstances, would have 'slipped away from God' (Johansson, 1924: 30). What happened was, after all, for the best, from Alma Johansson's missionary point of view. The fact that the Armenians were Christians was also important. She writes that it was easier to see Armenians 'fall into the hands of God than into the hands of human beings', and indicates that the outcome for other religious groups was uncertain (Johansson, 1930: 15). Her understanding of the events was obviously influenced by contemporary Christian thinking.

Western missionaries are often portrayed as assistants of colonialism. Through recent research, this image has become more nuanced as scholars have shown that at the same time as missionaries were an important part of imperialism, they also lived close to the local population and were influenced by their everyday encounters. Moreover, missionaries also contributed to social reforms and were often among the critics of colonial injustices (Etherington, 2005; Okkenhaug, 2003; Brown & Roger, 1999; Winks, 1999; Stanley, 1990). Alma Johansson can be interpreted as an example of such a missionary who was a link and negotiator between different cultures. One should not forget to take into consideration that she was Swedish and not from a colonial power. At the same time, Sweden was close to Germany, the ally of Turkey in this period. Alma Johansson cooperated with both German and other western missionaries, so the colonial link is evident in this sense.

In today's world of increasing globalisation and external interventions, it is important to reflect also on cultural encounters, and on the values that influence us and the values we create. The missionary writings about their work among people in foreign countries were very popular reading until well into the 20th century and coloured the readers' image of the world around them (Yegenouglu, 1998; Melman, 1995). Alma Johansson worked among the Christian minority of Armenians, but was also in contact with Muslim groups. Alma describes the encounter with the 'Other' in her writings and she then creates images of the 'Other'. From a close study of her texts I want to stress the human ambivalence.[10] On the one hand, Alma Johansson was part of contemporary Western Orientalism and spiritual imperialism when she expresses a depreciatory and prejudiced view of the 'Other'. On the other hand, she also describes a strong commitment and even understanding for the local population, both the Armenian and the Muslim, which should not be neglected.

In her writings Alma Johansson also describes how she feels exposed and vulnerable as a woman, even if she also shows great courage. This becomes evident in the violent world she lived and worked in. It is therefore essential also to dwell and reflect upon the images on the role of women in violent contexts and how this marks her writing.

Woman and civil actor in war

The traditional image of women in war is that of passive victims. They are massacred, bombed and raped. Women do not act, but react against the violence by creating strategies of survival and through care of others (Österberg & Lindstedt Cronberg, 2005: 234–37; Höglund, 2004; Goldman, 1998). These norms for femininities we also find in the texts by Alma.

In 1915, a typhus fever epidemic ravaged the region and many people died. The missionaries had a good reputation as medical orderlies and Alma Johansson and Bodil Biørn did what they could

---

10 See also my dissertation (Småberg 2005) for a developed discussion of ambivalent discourses and a model for interpretation including both dialogue and Orientalism.

in order to save lives. In this respect they answered to the female norm of nursing and caring. When the governor's sister became seriously ill, the governor called upon them. Since they thought the Armenians would benefit from it, they decided that Alma should undertake the commission (Johansson, 1930: 15).

The sister lived far away and the journey to get there was risky, especially for a woman, Alma Johansson points out: 'In the then circumstances it was more than ever fraught with danger for a lady to travel alone that far in the wilderness.' Together with her Armenian servant Michael, the town medical officer and a group of soldiers, she set out on a journey which would involve a snowstorm in the mountains and being lifted over precipices. Still, she thought that what was waiting for her upon arrival was far more frightening. She was very afraid of the husband of the sick woman, an official. The fear was that of being sexually abused: 'Each day the official came closer and he made it clear that he would not let me go back to Musch. I was filled with horror, when I understood that the doctor was on his side! I was careful though not to show my fears. But frightened I was indeed!' (Johansson, 1930: 16). The Muslim men were not to be trusted.

At the same time Alma Johansson heard how the men in the house discussed war rumours. They expressed hatred against Christians and took pleasure in telling about the violence against the Armenians in different places (Johansson, 1930: 17). On her way back home, she heard about the massacres of Armenians in Zeitun and Wan. Such information could be interpreted as early-warning signals today. Alma writes that the group of travellers became very excited and cheered by the news. Later in the spring, groups of women refugees arrived in her town, telling her and the other missionaries about the horrible things Turkish soldiers had subjected them to: 'Many times we just sat down with them crying'. They also tried to help 'while we still have time'. Already then they sensed that the catastrophe was also coming to Musch, but she writes: 'no one would think it was a planned slaughter from the highest quarters' (Johansson, 1930: 17–19). It is evident that in her opinion the massacres were organised from above and not merely unpredictably initiated locally.

She also shows how the civilians were affected, that the war did not only occur at the front but also in the local society. In this way, her story is a counter-narrative to the traditional image of the clearly defined war where soldiers fought each other and the civilians were situated at a safe distance. The Swedish historian Lina Sturfelt points out that the civilian and military, the front and the home, become especially blurred in the writings of the the First World War. In spite of this fact, Sturfelt shows that violence against women did not figure in the Swedish popular press during this period. Since the war was supposed to deal with male heroism, sacrifice and suffering, it was the male war victims who were made visible in the press, not the female. Alma Johansson's account of the civilian women therefore challenges, on another level, the prevailing gender order (Sturfelt, 2005: 234–37; Höglund, 2004; Kaldor, 1999).

Alma Johansson also describes how she, as an external actor, became a target. When the violence reached Musch, Alma tried to protect the orphanage through closing the gate, together with two other women. They then came under fire and the other women were hit. One of them died immediately, the other was badly wounded and died later among her friends inside the orphanage. Alma was then called upon to nurse two Muslims, among others, and she was forced to go into the street where the shootings went on. At the same time her colleague Bodil was ill with typhus fever, and at the orphanage Alma was needed more and more. Still she felt she needed to go: 'How we actually got there and then came home was a miracle; sometimes we had to crawl into a corner, when the bullets whistled around us. However, when you are in such a stressful situation, you become distanced to a certain degree to what is around you.'(Johansson, 1930: 25–30) Despite her vulnerable position, she nevertheless found the psychological strength to continue her work of helping others.

The exposed situation did not prevent her from trying to stand up for the Armenians and save the ones she could through negotiations; a means which is part of Ury's definition of the witness role (Ury, 2000). Many times soldiers came to search the orphanage. Alma Johansson then took on an advocate's role and made appeals for the village teachers who had been taken prisoner. She made it clear to the commandant that they were not deserters, but had legal papers to be there (Johansson, 1930: 25). On another occasion, their Albanian medical doctor, Dr Assaf, came after her, threatening to shoot her with his gun if she did not tell him where the Armenians were hiding. She refused, even though he put the gun to her breast and claimed that the orphanage had German connections: 'I told him to remember with whom he spoke. ... This was a *German* home.' (Johansson, 1930: 29). In this sense she claims the orphanage as a zone of peace/neutrality.

Alma Johansson also visited the governor to plead for the Armenians. She found him on a height where he led the firing on the town, and she was shocked by the way a human being can change in violent surroundings: 'I hope I will never see another person as devilish as the governor now was. We could not speak with him.' Instead she came into contact with an officer whom she perceived as 'very amiable'. He was understanding and promised that nothing would happen to the women and children. Alma trusted him: 'When such a man give us his word of honour and uses such language, how would I think that everything was a deceit'. She asked him to let her keep the teachers, but he answered that they could only keep three girls as maids and Alma's servant Michael: 'What could I do? I had to leave.' (Johansson, 1930: 29–30) Later, she also managed, against all odds, to save some of the surviving girls and take them with her home (Johansson, 1930: 34–35).

The Swedish historian David Gaunt stresses the difficulties which not only women but all external actors in Turkey faced when trying to stop the violence and help the victims. The genocide took place more or less in the open. The Allies – Britain, France and Russia – made a declaration that they would bring to trial those responsible for 'crimes against humanity and civilization'.[11] The threat, however, had no impact at all on Ottoman policy. Interventions by foreign diplomats were not tolerated or respected. Instead they were threatened or removed. This was also the fate of many Germans and Austrians who tried to intervene. Members of foreign religious missions, which often included medical doctors and nurses, were expressly prohibited and hindered from

---

11 This expression was coined in the Allies' declaration of May 20, 1915.

helping the deportees. Even the Red Cross was prohibited from entry (Gaunt, 2007).[12]

Today, actors in civil society are more and more in focus (Lederach, 1995; 1997; Kaldor, 2003). Focusing on previously neglected actors brings another level of understanding of peace activism and external interventions. Alma Johansson acted for the Armenians both by leaving her testimonies in order to reach out globally, and by undertaking humanitarian professional work locally. By studying an actor within civil society, I also want to indicate that initiatives that may seem harmless at first sight can be important, and to give them value. The Swedish historian Eva-Helen Ulvros argues that it is important to emphasise women and men who have acted locally for their visions of peace and justice, but lacked a national or international arena: 'As historians, we have a responsibility to make them come alive, bring them out from the shadows', Ulvros (2005: 202) writes. This is important, no matter whether they failed in bringing peace or saving lives, I hold.

In many contexts women have been excluded from official peace negotiations, but have nevertheless been active informally as advocates of non-violence and as builders of networks (Cockburn, 2007; Österberg & Lindstedt Cronberg, 2005; Meintjes, *et al.*, 2002; Andersson, 2001; Lorentzen & Turpin, 1998; Ruddick, 1989). In today's debate women's actions for peacebuilding are emphasised and there is a call to make more room for women in the official arena (UN Security Council resolution 2000). With this perspective in mind, it is interesting to view Alma Johansson as a woman and civil actor who steps out into the public to tell her story and takes a stand for the Armenians. She does so at a time when women's possibilities of independence were very limited. On becoming a missionary, Alma gets access to a world of more freedom of action. The American-Norwegian Peace and Conflict scholar Elise Boulding (1976) argues that women's traditionally marginalised role has given them the space to be creative and inventive, especially in the field of peacemaking. However, these contributions have often been

---

12 Gaunt shows many examples of foreigners who tried to intervene but failed.

overlooked. It is interesting to study how Alma Johansson stretches the boundaries of the gender norm while at the same time being defined/limited by it. Alma describes her exposed and vulnerable position as a woman. It becomes evident in her encounter with the Muslim world where she lives and works. At the same time, scholars argue that professional female missionaries from the West also became role-models to local women aiming to get a job (Hellesund & Okkenhaug, 2003; Chaudhuri & Strobel, 1992). Maybe Alma Johansson's commitment and appeals for a vulnerable people could also serve as a role-model.

Silence and speech

The Armenian genocide in 1915 has for a long time been met with silence. Sometimes it is called 'the forgotten genocide'. There are of course many reasons why the culture of silence has prevailed and why witnesses have not dared to, wanted to or had the strength to speak about their traumatic experiences. Alma Johansson, a Swedish witness to the massacres, decided to speak up and out, and to write her story.

'It is to the silence you should listen … What I have written is written between the lines', the Swedish poet Gunnar Ekelöf (1959) writes. Here I have tried to highlight Alma Johansson's perceptions of the Armenian genocide and the role she played as a witness. Within her story we find a willingness both to make the massacres known to the public, as well as to work on her experiences in writing. She then becomes an active witness. In the analysis of her texts, her role as a female missionary and civil actor in an armed conflict has been emphasised. In many ways a multifaceted and ambivalent story emerges which makes the unnoticed visible.

Alma Johansson describes her encounters with the local population and her view of the different people she meets. She is influenced by contemporary Western images of the Orient as an inferior civilisation and Christian views on Islam as something insufficient and degraded compared to Christianity. In her story, though, she differentiates between Muslims of various ethnicities and individualises them. They are not a large homogenous crowd which is dehumanised. Moreover, she describes how Turks are perpetrators, but also how they in some cases help and protect Armenians. The Armenians, both men and women, are passive victims, contrary to the official Turkish version in which they are regarded as rebellious and traitors. In her role as missionary, she is more of a humanitarian professional and development assistance worker than a colonial and Christian colporteur.

As a woman and civilian Alma Johansson describes herself as exposed and vulnerable, both physically and psychologically. She embarks on dangerous travels, feels sexually threatened; above all, she lives under siege and violence against civilians. It is evident for her that the violence is organised from above and can therefore be interpreted as genocide. She also shows that the war is not only at the front but also affects the civilians. Moreover, she makes women visible also as war victims in contrast to the traditional image of the fallen soldier. As a woman she stretches the gender norm pertaining to women in war even more when she is trying to resist the Turks' treatment of the Armenians. On the one hand she tries to make appeals, on the other hand she enters the public sphere to leave her report on the genocide. Alma Johansson always tried to safeguard the weak. In spite of all her ambiguity and ambivalence, Alma stands out. In the narrative her empathy for the exposed and her protest against the outrages is undivided.

CHAPTER 6

Sequencing of Peacemaking in Emerging Conflicts

Birger Heldt

Introduction

This broadly thematic book looks at roles and practices of external actors in different aspects of war and peace. This particular chapter places the issues in a global context by examining the patterns of third-party peacemaking in emerging intrastate armed conflicts from 1993 to 2004.

Third-party peacemaking is common and comes in many shapes and forms. Research has found that in the context of emerging intrastate armed conflicts some peacemaking tools are more efficient that others, whereas some are even detrimental in terms of reaching a negotiated end (Heldt, 2008b). One peacemaking tool may thus cancel out the positive impact of another tool rather than having a synergetic or multiplying effect. Meanwhile, the pattern of peacemaking in emerging conflicts is one of different tools applied seemingly at random. There is no orderly trajectory in that the peacemaking process moves from one tool to another, i.e., that it is sequenced.

The idea that different types of actions should be sequenced to

Acknowledgement. This chapter is a revised version of a paper presented at a workshop at the International Studies Association 49th Annual Convention, San Francisco, California (26–29 March, 2008), the Peace Research Institute of Oslo (PRIO) (15 May, 2008), the 2008 National Conference in Peace and Conflict Research, University of Lund (2–3 October, 2008) and at a workshop at Emory University (5–6 December, 2008). Comments from participants are gratefully acknowledged.

generate desired outcomes is common in many areas of research. For instance, there is an old debate on the necessity of sequencing democracy support (Berman, 2007; Carothers, 2007; Mansfield & Snyder, 2007). Mansfield and Snyder argue for sequencing, in that some cultural and socio-economic foundations for democracy should be at hand before the international community starts to support democratisation. In contrast, an approach labelled 'universalist' claims that there is no single path to – or preconditions for – democracy, but that it may arise in all sorts of ways (Berman, 2007). Timing and sequencing are here considered as inconsequential.

Considering that the notion of sequencing is widespread in different research communities, it is surprising to note that it is rarely raised in the context of peacemaking. Theoretically, properly sequenced peacemaking should have a higher success rate since it involves synergetic effects. As of yet, this compelling conjecture has not been exposed to statistical scrutiny. Focusing on the period 1993–2004, this chapter is a first cut at statistically assessing whether sequencing of peacemaking influences the probability of emerging intrastate armed conflicts ending through a ceasefire agreement or peace agreement. It reports findings that are overall supportive of the sequencing framework.

The second section of this chapter offers insight into the magnitude of the challenge by presenting basic empirical patterns on conflicts, peacemaking and the overall success rate. It attempts also to place these patterns in a wider context. The third section discusses the sequencing framework and formulates hypotheses on the impact of sequencing, whereas the fourth section presents some competing explanations of the negotiated termination of emerging armed conflicts. Statistical results are presented and discussed in the fifth section. The chapter concludes with some research- as well as policy-orientated implications in the sixth section.

Patterns of conflict and peacemaking

Whereas the number of civil conflicts has been almost constantly decreasing since the early 1990s, during the period 1993–2004 there were still 145 spells of conflict initiated (cf. Harbom, 2007).

Some of them were active in an on-and-off pattern in that they experienced several peace spells. Escalation to war took place in 35 cases, or about one third of all conflicts. In all but five of the cases escalating to war, escalation occurred within two calendar years. Escalation is thus in general imminent, and if a conflict has avoided escalation in the short-term, the risk of escalation plummets. This pattern may be due to the inherently most war-prone cases escalating right away, thus leaving the less war-prone cases behind. Another possible explanation is that peacemaking efforts start to bite – or are perhaps usually only initiated – after some period of time. As for the remaining conflicts, 18 of them ended through either a ceasefire agreement, partial or full peace agreement.[1] This leaves a bit more than half of the conflicts ending through victory, low activity, or censoring, by December 2004.

The armed conflicts in question are recently initiated low-level conflicts. From the concepts of 'ripeness' or 'hurting stalemate' (Zartman, 1985), or 'social' or 'event time' (Kleibor, 1996), we are led to expect challenges to achieving a breakthrough: the parties have not reached a standstill in fighting, nor been exposed to such a level of casualties that they have begun to consider settling the conflict at the negotiating table. In short, the conflict parties do not perceive any incentives for reaching an agreement as compared to continued conflict. To paraphrase Greig and Diehl (2006), the parties have not been 'softened up.' On the other hand, the limited duration and casualties may serve to make peace more likely (Greig, 2001; Greig & Diehl, 2006) as hostility levels are still low and memories of atrocities are limited. This should serve to make peacemaking more successful. In this scenario, casualties do not work as incentives but as disincentives for settlements.[2]

---

1 Data on conflict termination type is from Kreutz (2005).

2 Greig & Regan (2008), in a study covering the period 1944 to 1999, report that conflict duration (which to some extent should correlate with the cumulative number of battle deaths) has an inverted U-shaped curvilinear effect. The probability of accepting mediation at the start of the civil war initially increases, reaches a peak after 22 years, after which it decreases. Because civil wars reaching 22 years are rare, the finding means in practice that the prob-

Ackerman (2003: 340, 341) traces the idea of conflict prevention back to at least the Congress of Vienna in 1815, whereas the United Nations (UN) used the term 'preventive diplomacy' officially for the first time in 1960. The idea of prevention finally received prominence in the policy and research communities in the early 1990s. This coincided with a rising number of armed conflicts (cf. Harbom, 2007) as well as another role of third parties in armed conflict: peacekeeping operations in intrastate conflicts (cf. Heldt, 2008a). It appears fair to say that the 1990s were the decade when the international community's role and practice as a neutral third-party in armed conflicts went through an important change in terms of amount of action as well as its focus.

Considering this, it may not come as surprise that there was hardly a lack of peacemaking attempts in the mentioned conflicts. In this sample, mediation, good offices and third-party moderated direct talks took place some 700 times and were carried out by the UN, intergovernmental organisations (IGOs), states, non-governmental organisations (NGOs) or prominent persons.[3] With so many attempts there were on average 2.4 attempts per conflict year. While this figure may appear low, it is not clear how much higher it may be if individual attempts are not to overlap in time and thus potentially offset each other. Moreover, it not only takes time to carry out peacemaking attempts, but they also require time for preparations. Nevertheless, so many attempts, and so few suc-

---

ability of accepting mediation offers are increasing throughout civil wars. This is in turn supportive of the 'ripe moment' argument. It is, however, unclear whether willingness to accept mediation correlates with the probability of reaching an agreement. It is possible that as the willingness to talk increases, the probability of reaching an agreement decreases as the willingness to compromise is reduced.

3 Good offices involve a third-party offering conflict parties an opportunity and venue to meet and communicate directly by providing location, facilities, etc. In third-party aided direct talks the parties meet face-to-face, but an interlocutor is present and takes a more active part in the talks than during good offices. Mediation involves indirect communication through an intermediary. Data is from the FBA/UCDP Managing Intrastate Low-level Conflict (MILC) dataset, 1993–2004 (version 1.0).

cesses, mean that there were on average 40 peacemaking attempts for every breakthrough; a success rate of about 2.5%. Regardless of whether emerging conflicts are inherently difficult to deal with, the success rate can be regarded as disappointing. The success rate is also a sobering reminder of how difficult it is to succeed with peacemaking, and should serve to generate realistic expectations among third parties concerning what they may expect to achieve. It should also serve to generate profound thoughts on how much the art of peacemaking can and should be improved.

When reflecting on this success rate, it is important to get some perspective by keeping the medical sciences in mind. It is widely held that the social sciences (and thus in extension the practice of peacemaking) – for reasons of the alleged outstanding complexity of social phenomena – will never reach the accuracy of the medical sciences. But as Stern and Druckman note (2000: 34):

> In fact, medical science is finding that few diseases follow this model. Smallpox and yellow fever may, but cancer may be a more apt analogy for international conflict. There are many types of cancer, many paths the disease may take through time, and many points at which medical intervention may do some good. As with international conflict, the multifaceted nature of cancer makes it very hard to understand and treat.

Just like conflicts, some diseases are difficult to predict and prevent, as their causes are to varying extent unknown. For some diseases, an increased cure rate from 10% to 25% may be hailed as a breakthrough. Another fact is that it was only by the beginning of the 20th century that the medical sciences, after hundreds of years of research and practice, had progressed to the point that it had become more likely that a visit to a doctor in the US would make the patient less ill instead of causing harm (Hardin, 2002: 183). With this in mind, and considering that peacemaking is a recent and difficult practice, and an even more recent research area, its success rate should cause neither surprise nor pessimism.

Sequencing theory and peacemaking

Planning and implementing a strategy is like preparing a recipe for a special dish, or the formula for dynamite. Do something at the wrong time, or put things together in the wrong sequence, and you could end up with a disaster, even though the right things were done, or the correct ingredients were used (Cohen, 2004: 148).

It is generally held that the choice of peacemaking tool should be conditioned by the conflict phase (e.g., Lund, 2008), but it is difficult to come by details of what this means in concrete terms. As noted by Hampson (2002: 153), the literature is rather quiet on the issue of proper tools and sequencing of peacemaking. A rare exception is Wall and Stark (1996) who discuss sequencing of mediation strategies of a specific tool, which over time should be applied in a certain order to increase the likelihood for success. Sequencing may also refer to the order of different tools such as mediation, good offices, and third-party moderated direct talks. Given the different characteristics of peacemaking tools, it appears inconceivable that the choice of tool is inconsequential for the outcome.

Third-party attempts are supposed to move the process forward by softening up the parties, increasing mutual trust and negotiating skills, and providing information on fundamental issues that make parties more likely to spot zones of agreements (e.g., Bercovitch & Gartner, 2006; Greig & Diehl, 2006). Sequencing – whether in terms of strategies or tools – implies that early efforts may, or perhaps even should, fail to generate a breakthrough, but they will inch the process forward, which the next attempt can build upon. Quick breakthroughs should thus not be expected. Ultimately, an attempt with another peacemaking tool will tip the scale as it builds on previous attempts. This means that initial steps can only have indirect effects, and that only the last tool will have a direct and decisive effect. Weak or no direct effects of some tools/attempts, especially if the sequencing history of a case has not been taken into account, should therefore be expected if the tools are located at the beginning of the sequence. In methodological terms the sequencing framework implies thus that to assess the effectiveness of a particular peacemaking tool, the history of peacemaking must be controlled for. The aforementioned low overall average direct effectiveness of peacemaking may thus be explained by either a combination of these implications, or because sequencing did not take place.

Empirically, peacemaking is seldom sequenced in this orderly manner. As an illustration, consider the conflict between the government of Bosnia and Herzegovina and the insurgent Croat Republic of Bosnia and Herzegovina in 1993. During just the last three months of 1993, mediation (M), third-party moderated direct talks (D) and good offices (G) were initiated in the following sequence: M, D, G, G, D, D, G, G, G, G, D, D, G, D, M, D, D, D, G, D, G, D, G, G, D, M, D, G, G, M, D, G, G, G, M, D, G, G, M, M, G, G.[4] Over the entire year a grand total of 84 peacemaking attempts were launched. By simple visual inspection it is difficult to discern any single strategy, let alone any element of sequencing. It is also difficult to understand how one peacemaking attempt may try to build on previous attempts, or even how the conflict actors themselves can keep up with the process and even take it seriously as a whole. This is especially so since although peacemaking attempts had different start dates, they were sometimes ongoing simultaneously, i.e., they were overlapping. It is not implausible that this peacemaking pattern may have prolonged the conflict. In the end, the conflict was solved on the battlefield instead of through negotiations.

It appears reasonable to expect that any third-party will have a consistent peacemaking strategy for a certain case in terms of a specific tool. It is simply difficult to believe that third parties change peacemaking tool from one attempt to another, and then back again, within short time intervals in a specific conflict. The multitude of peacemaking tools applied in a seemingly chaotic pattern in individual cases should thus be a consequence of at best complementary – or at worst uncoordinated and even competitive – peacemaking efforts by several third parties. In the Bosnian case there were twelve third parties involved, but that counts only those that pursued any of the three previously mentioned peacemaking tools. Third-party intervention involving more than one third-party may thus by its

---

4 Data is from the FBA/UCDP Managing Intrastate Low-level Conflict (MILC) dataset, 1993–2004 (version 1.0).

nature be inconsistent (Kriesberg, 1996; Heldt, 2008b) and for that reason also open to manipulation by conflict parties as it allows them to 'shop around' or wait for better deals, or even play out the third parties against one another in search of a better deal or to sabotage peacemaking attempts (Heldt, 2008b).

Other scholars, too, have suggested a cumulative effect of peacemaking, but they have reached the conclusion from other theoretical vantage points and with varying degrees of empirical success (e.g., Bercovitch & Gartner, 2006; Greig & Diehl, 2006; Heldt, 2008b; Regan & Aydin, 2006; Regan & Stam, 2000). They have also focused on the cumulative effect of a specific peacemaking tool instead of the cumulative effect of the overall and sequenced process. Regan and Stam (2000) focus on the interstate militarised dispute month and attempt to predict dispute duration. A dispute is coded as having ended regardless of whether it involves low activity, settlement, or even victory for one of the parties. A negative relationship is reported between the number of mediation attempts by the same actor and dispute duration. Using the mediation attempt as unit of analysis, Greig (2001) focuses on enduring interstate rivalries, which refer to dyadic disputes that have lasted at least twenty years and gone through at least six dispute spells. The study is limited to disputes involving at least one mediation attempt. Greig reports a negative relationship between the total number of mediation attempts and full/partial agreements in interstate enduring rivalries. No effect is identified for the number of mediation attempts by the same mediator. Greig interprets the finding as showing a selection effect: the more difficult the case, the more mediation attempts. Meanwhile, Heldt (2008b) focuses on conflict resolution in terms of negotiated ends in a context of emerging (rather than enduring) intrastate (rather than interstate) conflicts, and reports a positive relationship between the total number of mediation attempts as well as third-party moderated direct talks, and the likelihood of negotiated resolutions. The cumulative impact of good office attempts is meanwhile found to be strongly negative.

Sequencing in theory: Four testable implications

The sequencing framework does not offer more than ordering key concepts and a basic assumption. While valuable as a point of departure, the framework does not generate insights into what and how tools should be ordered. An auxiliary theory/assumption is therefore necessary in order to generate hypotheses that can be used for assessing the framework.

A point of departure for differentiating and ordering peacemaking tools is the auxiliary assumption that unaided direct talks between parties in emerging conflicts are least likely to succeed (cf. Heldt, 2008b). Briefly, the parties have recently ended up in armed conflict, and this reflects an inability to successfully carry out direct talks in the immediate past. If direct dialogue has failed in the recent past, and after armed conflict has commenced, then one should hold it unlikely that the parties can achieve a breakthrough by themselves. In short, emerging armed conflicts reflect that the parties – for reasons of distrust, overblown optimism on the likelihood of victory and/or lack of negotiation skills – are unable to solve their differences on their own.

For emerging conflicts this suggests that third-party peacemaking tools will have a synergetic or multiplier effect provided they are sequenced according to the extent they allow the parties to communicate directly. Good offices are located at one end of the continuum. They offer conflict parties an opportunity and venue to meet and communicate directly. Third parties do not actively engage in, or moderate, the talks but only facilitate talks by providing location, facilities, etc. Third-party aided direct talks constitute a middle category in terms of direct communication between conflict parties. Parties meet face-to-face, but an interlocutor is present and takes a more active part in the talks than during good offices. Aided talks create some distance between the parties as the dialogue is moderated by a third-party. Mediation is located at the other end of the continuum. It involves indirect communication through an intermediary. Mediators are bringing messages from one party to the other, trying to assist the parties to reach an agreement by making them see issues in another light, sorting out misunderstandings, formulate positions, or even offer political and economic rewards for concessions. Mediation may thus involve communication, facilitation, or even manipulation by the third-party (Quinn *et al.*, 2006). This analysis suggests that in emerging conflicts mediation should ideally be applied first, followed by third-party aided direct talks, after which good offices should be applied.

H.1. If applied after mediation, there is a positive relationship between good offices and negotiated ends of emerging intrastate armed conflicts.

H.2 If applied after mediation, there is a positive relationship between third-party moderated direct talks and negotiated ends of emerging intrastate armed conflicts.

H.3 If applied after third-party moderated direct talks, there is a positive relationship between good offices and negotiated ends of emerging intrastate armed conflicts.

Apart from overall order, sequencing also implies something about the consistency of sequences. Whereas one tool may overall have been applied after another tool, it may not have been applied in an undisturbed sequence. Instead there may exist a considerable degree of overlap. The sequencing framework implies that the less overlap of a series of attempts by a certain tool, the stronger the impact of the tool in question.

H.4 There is a positive relationship between the non-overlap of a peacemaking sequence and negotiated ends of emerging intrastate armed conflicts.

Competing explanations
Number of peacemaking attempts

As mentioned above, some theoretical approaches focus on the cumulative amount of peacemaking efforts rather than the sequence of peacemaking efforts. As the argument goes, every peacemaking attempt sets a precedent, in that it hopefully moves the process forwards, on which the next attempt can build (e.g., Regan & Stam, 2000; Heldt, 2008b; Greig & Regan, 2008). Regan and Stam and Greig and Regan conjecture that a cumulative effect is at hand to the extent that the same mediator carries out mediation, whereas Heldt focuses on the cumulative amount of peacemaking efforts irrespective of the number of mediators. The common thread, however, is the argument that regardless of whether past efforts moved the process forwards, they convey information to the conflict parties that will in turn enable them to identify areas of agreement. Partly in line with this, it is proposed that as the number of third-party peacemaking attempts accumulates, so will also the capital of peace.

As mentioned above, third-party peacemaking tools can be ordered according to the extent they allow face-to-face communication. Good offices are located at one end of the continuum, moderated direct talks are in the middle, whereas mediation is located at the other end. Recalling the above arguments, we are led to believe that in and by itself, good offices will be the least successful strategy, and may even be detrimental. The reason is that it allows for direct communication, whereas the conflict parties are not able to handle it in this early conflict phase unless it follows upon the application of some peacemaking tools that involve indirect communication. In contrast, moderated direct talks create some distance between the parties, as their encounters are moderated and directed by a third-party. There are then reasons to believe that such talks will be beneficial in these types of conflicts. Thirdly and finally, there is mediation, which involves the conflict parties communicating through an intermediary. Since mediation creates minimum direct interaction, we are led to expect that mediated talks will have a positive impact on the probability for a negotiated settlement, and that the impact may be stronger than for third-party aided direct talks.

> H.5 There is no, or even a negative, relationship between the cumulative amount of good offices and negotiated ends of emerging intrastate armed conflicts.

> H.6 There is a positive relationship between the cumulative amount

of third-party moderated direct talks and negotiated ends of emerging intrastate armed conflicts.

H.7 There is a positive relationship between the cumulative amount of mediation attempts and negotiated ends of emerging intrastate armed conflicts.

Conflict issue

Incompatible positions over the allocation of territory (i.e., the parties' demands concern either border adjustments or the distribution of territories) are commonly claimed to constitute close to a necessary condition for interstate war (Heldt, 1999; Goertz & Diehl, 1992; Kocs, 1995; Huth, 1996; Vasquez & Henehan, 2001). A similar importance of territory can be observed in intrastate wars and armed conflicts short of war. In these cases rebels demand autonomy or independence. Another issue in intrastate wars and armed conflicts is government, in that one party demands partial or total government control and/or change of the political system. In a similar manner the Brahimi report (United Nations, 2000: 4) conjectures that 'political and economic objectives may be more fluid and open to compromise than objectives related to [...] ethnicity [...].' Similar claims can be found in, e.g., Diehl (1994: 174). This implies that conflicts over territory are less amenable to successful peacemaking than conflicts over government.

H.8 Emerging intrastate armed conflicts over territory are less likely than conflicts over government to end through negotiation.

Conflict history

Part of the general idea of an impact of historical experiences, is the common claim that the history of relations, with regard to war and peace, between two parties has implications for future relations. Jackman (1999) claims that '[...] each unit's history can be used to generate forecasts for that unit, [...]' because '[...] past conflict (or the absence of past conflict) are potentially valuable signals [...]' that parties '[...] use to update their beliefs about the type of a dyad partner, information that [...]' is used '[...] in choosing strategies in the current time period.' (Jackman, 1999: 8). Similar to this, Crescenzi and Enterline (2001: 410–411) argue that 'the claim that history is relevant to future interstate relations is perhaps obvious to the point of triviality', and 'the occurrence of co-operation between two states at time t, for example, conditions the likelihood that cooperation will occur at time t + n.' Following Roe (2000: 189) who quotes Posen, this line of reasoning can be expressed in a more straightforward manner: 'When groups make judgements of others' intentions '[t]he main mechanism they will use is history: how did the other group behave last time [...]'' This theme is also part of the concept of 'enduring rivalry', the impact of which has been studied extensively (Goertz & Diehl, 2000).

Failed peace spells will thus serve to make a negotiated end more difficult to achieve. In this conception, beliefs about future co-operation or non-cooperation are not influenced by an analysis of whether future co-operation by an actor would be rational given some specific interest or preference, and related payoffs of co-operating or defecting, of that actor.

> H.9 There is a negative relationship between past conflict spells and negotiated ends of emerging intrastate armed conflicts.

Sequencing in practice: The historical pattern

For the purpose of statistical analysis a dataset was created that contains all minor armed conflict dyads 1993–2004 as identified in Harbom (2007), and the unit of analysis is the minor armed conflict dyad year. By minor armed conflict is meant a conflict dyad between a government and an organised actor, where the issue fought over concerns either government (power itself, the composition of government) or territory (independence or autonomy), where the annual number of battle deaths is at least 25, and has never in the past reached the level of 1000 per year (Ibid.). Of all conflict spells, only those that were initiated during the period are selected, and this generates 145 spells. The reason for including only conflicts initiated during the period concerns measurement: for spells that started before 1993 there is no data on peacemaking, and the peacemaking history can thus not be measured. Finally, because conflict spells are of different duration due to different starting dates, censoring, escalation to war, low activity or negotiated ends, the dataset constitutes an unbalanced time series pool. Eighteen conflict spells ended by negotiation. A negotiated end means that the conflict is inactive because of either a ceasefire agreement, a partial peace agreement (leaving some issues unresolved to be addressed at a later stage) or a comprehensive peace agreement (Bercovitch & Gartner, 2006). Unresolved conflicts may be terminated because of low activity, escalation to war, or victory for any party.

A summary of the statistical findings is found in table 1.[5] It shows that the relative timing of good offices vis-à-vis moderated direct talks ('Direct Talks >Good Offices') is inconsequential: good offices can be applied before direct talks, or after, with no difference in terms of the impact on the likelihood of a negotiated end. Meanwhile, the relative timing of good offices vis-à-vis mediation matters ('Mediation >Good Offices'): if good offices as hypothesised are on average applied after mediation, a negotiated end is on average more than eleven times more likely as compared to when good offices are applied not at all, or before, mediation. The relative timing of direct talks vis-à-vis mediation matters too ('Mediation >Direct Talks'): if third-party moderated direct talks as hypothesised are applied after mediation, a negotiated end is on average more than seven times more likely as compared to when direct talks are applied not at all, or before, mediation.

---

5 The statistical findings build on multivariate Cox regression analysis of annual survival time data. Detailed statistical results as well as information on data and measurement are available on request from the author.

Table I. Predicting the negotiated termination of emerging intrastate conflicts, 1993–2004

Factor	Direction of impact	Size of impact
Direct Talks >Good Offices	none	n.a.
Mediation >Good Offices	positive	+ 1139%
Mediation >Direct Talks	positive	+ 746%
Mediation overlap	none	n.a.
Direct Talks overlap	none	n.a.
Good Offices overlap	none	n.a.
Mediation (cumulative)	positive	+ 166%
Direct Talks (cumulative)	positive	+ 22%
Good Offices (cumulative)	negative	- 81%
Previous Conflict	negative	- 74%*
Territorial Conflict	none	n.a.

* The p-value barely exceeds the 0,05 threshold and is 0,06.

This difference in effect may be claimed to be consistent with the sequencing framework. If third-party moderated direct talks are more similar to mediation, than are good offices in terms of the degree to which they offer the conflict parties an opportunity for direct communication, proper sequencing of good offices is more critical than the proper sequencing of direct talks. If it is more critical, it should also make a greater difference in terms of the effect on the likelihood of negotiated ends. Meanwhile, the absence of impact from sequencing concerning good offices vis-à-vis third-party talks becomes difficult to explain with the same line of argument, i.e., that the absence of impact may be due to a too small difference between these tools in terms of the degree to which they allow conflict parties to communicate directly. The reason is that such a claim would be inconsistent with the first claim that implies a substantial difference (i.e., that proper sequencing of good offices is more critical than proper sequencing of direct talks). A more developed theory and more empirical research is needed to sort out this empirical anomaly.

As indicated by the variables 'Mediation overlap', 'Direct Talks overlap' and 'Good Offices overlap', the statistical analysis is unable to unearth an effect of the tightness of sequencing: hence, and surprisingly, the degree of overlap between peacemaking tools does not matter. It is not decisive to get sequencing perfectly right (i.e., no overlap among peacemaking tools). The process of peacemaking appears thus to be insensitive to transgressions from perfect sequencing. This insight carries important policy implications.

As for the competing explanations, table I shows that every moderated direct talk increases the probability of a negotiated settlement by on average 22%, whereas every mediated talk increases the probability by on average 166%. In other words, one mediation attempt corresponds to eight third-party moderated talks, everything else being equal. Repeated mediation attempts will thus make a substantial contribution. This means that apart from creating conditions for the success of moderated direct talks, mediation has a direct positive impact by itself. Mediation does then not necessarily have to be followed by moderated direct talks to be beneficial. Meanwhile, every good office attempt decreases the probability of a negotiated end by on average 81%. Repeated good offices attempts will thus sharply diminish the likelihood of a negotiated end. This means in practice that it requires on average one mediation attempt – or eight direct talks – to offset the on average damaging impact of two good office attempts.

As for the remaining control variables, the impact of past conflict is bordering on statistical significance: if conflict parties have been involved in at least one conflict spell in the past, the likelihood of a negotiated end drops by 74%. This indicates the importance of reaching a negotiated end of the first spell, as conflicts that become dormant to later reappear will become even more difficult to manage. One finding contradicts a widely-held view: conflict type does not matter. Conflicts over territory are not less likely to end through negotiation than conflicts over government.

Overall, these findings indicate that there are two pathways to generate a negotiated end to violence. Numerous or non-sequenced peacemaking attempts can substitute for an orderly and sequenced peacemaking process, just as an orderly peacemaking process can substitute for numerous peacemaking attempts. However, the table shows that it takes on average thirty-four instances of third-party moderated direct talks, or more than on average four mediation attempts, to match the average impact of a properly sequenced process in which moderated direct talks are applied after mediation. Meanwhile, emerging conflicts, when they escalate to war, do so almost always within at most twenty-four months. A non-sequenced approach will thus take longer time to reach fruition, simply because a large number of peacemaking attempts requires a lot of time to implement. This means that a non-sequenced approach may not be able to generate a sufficient amount of attempts in such a short period of time in order to be preferable to a sequenced approach. The optimal approach is then to combine sequencing with non-sequencing: start by carrying out a couple of mediation attempts as quickly as possible, then switch towards moderated direct talks to create an additional large boost of 700% in the likelihood of a negotiated end. Eventually, conflict parties will almost by definition also have to face one another to finalise an agreement.

On a final methodological note, it is often pointed out that a selection effect may be at work: mediation is not randomly assigned to conflicts. On the one hand, mediators may select the 'easy' cases (Svensson, 2007) where there is some/high chance of success. On the other hand, mediators may be handed the most difficult and hopeless cases. Empirical evidence suggests that mediators end up handling cases with the lowest likelihood for resolution (Greig, 2005; Svensson, 2007). This 'adverse' (Svensson, 2007) selection process means that the peacemaking measures here studied had the odds stacked against them, but still (in two instances) managed to have a positive impact. While the precise magnitude of this selection effect needs to be calculated, it means that all coefficients here reported have been exposed to a downward – not upward – bias. It also means that if the selection effect had been incorporated into the statistical model, the coefficients would have changed to an unknown magnitude in a positive direction. Whether incorporation of the selection effect would lead to the effect of good offices changing from negative to positive cannot be determined beforehand. Yet it is doubtful whether this would be the case, considering the large change that is required for this coefficient to become statistically significant and positive.

Final reflections

The findings in this chapter are supportive of the peacemaking sequencing framework. They suggest that conflict parties in early conflict phases should not in general be encouraged to carry out unaided face-to-face meetings; neither should third parties in general offer good offices. Conflict parties should instead ideally first communicate indirectly a couple of times through a third-party, and thereafter carry out third-party moderated direct talks. The findings suggest also that the effect of peacemaking tools is cumulative, and this means that mediation and direct talks in the early phases of conflicts are less likely than later attempts to become successful. This insight carries important methodological as well as policy orientated implications.

Apart from assessing the robustness of these findings with the help of additional control variables, future research would do well to improve the basic theoretical framework of sequencing. There is a need for a more detailed theory offering a more detailed account of the 'why' and 'how' of sequencing. At present, the sequencing argument is little more than a theoretical framework, the details of which need to be worked out to offer a more profound understanding of the mechanism at work. A possible way forward is to combine the sequencing framework with more developed theories instead of creating a new theory of sequencing. This could help not only to generate additional hypotheses, but may also assist in modelling test equations and measurement, as well as an increased ability to formulate more finely-tuned policy implications.

Turning to policy implications, and considering that emerging conflicts are especially prone to escalate to war in the very early stages, the findings indicate a severe challenge for early action: while it is important to act early, early action (because of the cumulative impact as well as sequencing) is less successful in reaching a negotiated end than late action. This insight highlights how important it is that the international community identifies ways to co-ordinate peacemaking, as this is a precondition for proper sequencing. Because of the historically high risk of immediate escalation to civil war, there is a need for a system or template for coordination of peacemaking that will work from the very first days of an emerging conflict and achieve immediate results. There is no time for creating coordination once a conflict has arisen. In short, there is a need for a new and more strategic and coordinated practice. At the same time the UN has since the mid-1990s worked to improve coordination of peacekeeping and peacemaking with regional actors (Heldt, 2008a: 9).

Because of the urgency of peacemaking, coordination appears to have to involve a predetermined third-party that (with the support of the international community) takes the overall responsibility for an individual emerging conflict. The UN and some IGOs (regional as well as sub-regional) such as the European Union (EU), the Organisation for Security and Cooperation in Europe (OSCE) or the Organisation of American States (OAS), appear to be the only viable and legitimate actors to effectively assume such regional responsibilities. At the same time, such ideal planning would be extremely difficult or even utopian to achieve and also to implement in some regions of the world where 'region' is not synonymous with 'community', because of vested interests among some countries or because of festering latent/manifest interstate conflicts in these regions. New thinking is needed among practitioners and researchers on how best to address such issues in regions where coordination problems may be foreseen.

CHAPTER 7

Mediating between Tigers and Lions
Norwegian Peace Diplomacy in Sri Lanka's Civil War

Kristine Höglund & Isak Svensson

Introduction

Sri Lanka has suffered from one of Asia's most intractable civil wars. The official abrogation of the Ceasefire Agreement (CFA) in January, 2008, marked the definitive end to the latest attempt to settle the conflict. During this peace attempt, Norway functioned as a mediator between the government of Sri Lanka – representing a country with the Lion as a national symbol – and the Liberation Tigers of Tamil Eelam (LTTE).[1] Norway received both praise and criticism for its involvement. They were applauded for brokering the ceasefire agreement, which to a considerable extent ended direct confrontation between the parties for several years. However, the Norwegian mediators were seen as too lax in their responses to the human rights abuses committed, both by the government and the rebels, and have been perceived as having a too passive approach to their third-party effort.

Why did Norway – despite having no obvious national or security

---

Acknowledgement. This chapter is also to be published as an article bearing the same title in *Contemporary South Asia* 2009, Vol. 17: 2. Reprinted with permission by the publisher Taylor and Frenas.

1 The majority community of Sri Lanka are called 'Sinhalese' – from 'Sinha', the Sinhalese word for lion – meaning descended from a lion. The separatist group, the Liberation Tigers of Tamil Eelam (LTTE), make use of the tiger as a symbol.

concerns – become involved in the Sri Lankan conflict? And what are the implications of Norway as a mediator, and its mediation style for the process and outcome of the negotiations? In this article, we explore the rationale behind Norwegian involvement, and how the mediation effort has been influenced by regional and global dynamics.[2] This analysis focuses on the national and regional causes, and consequences of the Norwegian intervention, rather than Norway's internal dynamics.[3] We argue that Norway's aspiration to promote an image of being a global peacemaker was important in explaining its willingness to take on the role as a mediator in Sri Lanka. The consent required from regional and global powers for intervention in Sri Lanka is critical for understanding why Norway, and not another state or organisation, became involved. What is important in this regard is that the international campaign against terrorism has had a substantial impact on the size of the pool of potential mediators, and the space for peace negotiations between governments and non-state armed groups. Moreover, the Norwegian approach to mediation in Sri Lanka – based on impartiality, emphasising ownership of the process by the primary parties, and seeking a high degree of internationalisation – had implications for how the process unfolded.

Exploring the Sri Lankan case enhances the theoretical understanding of the issue of mediation selection in internal armed conflict, and its linkages to regional and global processes. Our analytical point of departure is the assumption that states – and we restrict our attention to states in this study – basically pursue mediation as a policy tool for the advancement of specific interests. While some studies address questions related to the motives of mediators, few

2 This study is informed by fieldwork in Sri Lanka (December 2002, November 2003, January 2006, December 2006, September and November/December 2007) and Norway (February and April 2008), including interviews with for example, Norwegian officials, representatives of the Tamil Diaspora, and analysts of the peace process. We acknowledge generous funding from Sida/ Sarec and the Swedish Research Council.

3 In this sense we recognise that there have been different perspectives in Norway's approach in Sri Lanka between, for instance, Norway's Foreign Ministry, Norad and the Non-Governmental Organisational sector, yet we treat Norway as a unitary actor.

have explored the connection between motives and the implications for mediation success (Touval, 2003). This study contributes to this unexplored, but important, discourse.

Norway gained official recognition for its peace efforts in Sri Lanka in late 1999, when President Kumaratunga publicly announced Norway's status as a facilitator. This was in an attempt to explore an end to the conflict with the LTTE. Norway, and the parties to the conflict, refer to its intervention as 'facilitation'; a term which is often used to denote a less intrusive form of intervention than mediation. In this article, we use the terms mediation and mediator to describe the Norwegian activities, while facilitation is conceptualised as a sub-category of activities among the mediator's activities. These distinctions will be explored more fully in the subsequent sections.

The Sri Lankan state-formation conflict has its origin in competing forms of nationalism: the Sinhalese and the Tamil state-formation projects (Uyangoda, 2007a). The Sinhalese majority had felt discriminated during British rule, and perceived their traditional religion and society as threatened. Therefore, a Sinhalese political nationalism developed that initiated reforms which prioritised the Sinhalese community over the Tamil minority (DeVotta, 2007; Thambiah, 1992).[4] In response, the Tamils mobilised, first politically, and eventually militarily. In the mid-1970s the separatist LTTE, along with other Tamil militant groups, were formed and the conflict escalated into civil war in the 1980s (Wilson, 2000). Several attempts to resolve the conflict have been made, of which the most recent peace process, in 2002–2008, is the focus of this study. A combination of internal factors, such as war-weariness and regime change, and external factors, such as the changing international climate in the wake of 9/11, facilitated the initiation of the peace process.[5] Yet the

---

4 The Sinhalese constitute around 74% of the 18 million people in Sri Lanka. The Tamils are the second largest group, around 18%. The Muslims make up some 7%, are Tamil speaking, and see themselves as a distinct ethnic group.

5 To monitor the ceasefire, an international peace mission was created: the Sri Lanka Monitor Mission (SLMM). The SLMM consisted of monitors from only Nordic countries (Norway, Sweden, Denmark, Finland and Iceland). The head

history of the conflict shows that negotiations, through direct talks or mediation, have shown themselves to have little effect on these underlying dynamics and have, instead, become part of the contention (Philipson, 2001). Furthermore, the failed peace process added to the complexity of the conflict, as well as the hostility between the main parties (Uyangoda, 2007a). At the same time, due to the intractability of the conflict, the need for third-party mediation has often been stressed in the Sri Lankan context.

The Norwegian mediators performed several important functions in the peace process. Norway's role was mainly to facilitate the process; to 'assist the parties' in the peace efforts. To this end they have served as a channel for communication between the parties, either as a messenger in shuttle diplomacy, or in facilitating direct meetings. They assisted in the drafting of agendas and documents. Norway was also instrumental in finding venues for the six rounds of peace talks that were held between September 2002 and March 2003, and for the additional rounds of talks that were held in efforts to save the peace process. Moreover, Norway has been an important player in garnering international support for the peace process. As one of the donor co-chairs – next to the United States (US), the European Union (EU) and Japan – the Norwegian mediators have sought to convince the international community to commit funds for reconstruction and development. Hence Norway played a key role in the peace efforts in Sri Lanka. To explain why Norway was involved, and the mediation approaches taken by this mediator, is therefore important if we seek a deeper understanding of the dynamics of the now failed peace process.

This study proceeds in four sections. First, we discuss the theoretical debate on why certain third parties offer, and why belligerents request, mediation in violent conflicts. Secondly, we explore the Norwegian approach to peacemaking and its motives for engaging in Sri Lanka. In essence, we discuss how the occurrence of Norwegian mediation was a function of local, regional and global

---

of the mission was to be appointed by Norway, also placing it at the core of the monitoring function. The SLMM served in Sri Lanka until January, 2008 when the Sri Lankan Government formally declared the ceasefire void.

power-dynamics. Thirdly, we explore the implications of the Norwegian mediation on the conflict dynamics in Sri Lanka. We end by discussing the conclusions.

Mediation: Motives and selection

Mediation is based on non-coercive engagement with the contestant parties and involves a series of activities to manage or solve a conflict. Some scholars make a distinction between facilitation and mediation as two types of third-party intervention, where facilitation (or conciliation) is seen as a method mainly aimed at assisting in communication between the parties (e.g. Fischer and Keashly, 1991). However, facilitation is commonly seen as one task a mediator can perform, along with activities such as drafting of proposals, building trust between the belligerents, managing the process, and coordinating concessions (e.g. Bercovitch, 2002). In this article, facilitation is seen as a sub-set of activities in third-party mediation.

Mediation is only one form of third-party intervention in promoting peacemaking. Compared to military intervention, mediation and diplomacy are relatively inexpensive policy tools. Nonetheless, for the state, or organisation engaged in mediation activities, mediation carries costs, both in resources and potential loss in prestige. Why, then, do mediators get involved?

The motive of the mediator

The motives of the mediators depend on a set of parameters. This study is concerned with the mediation of states, and views mediation as a foreign policy instrument that states have at hand. While studies on mediator motives recognise the political considerations as a driving force in mediation, Saadia Touval argued that the implications of this fact have rarely been discussed: '... after stating that mediation is initiated for political purposes, mediation theory takes over. Analyses usually do not follow up on the premise that political purposes generate mediation, instead proceeding to discuss and evaluate it in terms of a prescriptive theory of mediation' (2003: 91). Thus it is important to scrutinize the political purposes behind mediation attempts in order to examine the extent to which the objective is related to the conflict itself, or rather, is found in dynamics beyond the conflict.

There have been several attempts to categorise the driving motives behind mediation (e.g. Mitchell, 1988; Touval & Zartman, 2001). In this article we distinguish between motives related to three different sources from which mediation rewards arise: rewards relating to the conflict itself; rewards emerging from the domestic constituency, and rewards found in the international and regional context.[6]

Requesting external mediation

Entering into an internal conflict by a mediator is not only dependent on the mediator's willingness to intervene, but also on the belligerents' acceptance of mediation in general, and specifically of a certain mediator (Betts, 1999; Crocker, Hampson & Aall, 2004). For the primary parties, there are certain benefits in accepting mediation. First of all, the parties may be stuck in what has been denoted a 'mutually hurting stalemate' and seek ways to escape this costly deadlock (Zartman, 2000). What is important in this regard is a perception that the parties cannot settle the conflict by themselves (Pruitt & Kim, 2004). The belligerents will be more open to outside assistance if previous efforts without the help of external mediators have been ineffective. Secondly, the government, as well as the rebels, may have a sense of optimism about the potential to reach mutually beneficial solutions to the conflict, which may affect their choice of mediator. In this sense, if the mediators are associated with a possibility to find a 'way out' or an 'enticing opportunity', this can make mediation more attractive than a continuation of the armed struggle (Ohlson, 1998; Zartman, 2000). There are also other motives for accepting third-party mediation – such as a wish to re-group and re-arm, internationalize the conflict, or search for legitimization – which may complement, but sometimes override, concerns about ending the conflict (Richmond, 1998).

In internal armed conflicts, there are also basic asymmetries

---

6 Our ideas build on Mitchell (1988).

that influence the selection of mediators. The government side has power dominance in terms of legitimacy and international recognition. For this reason, it is costly to engage in official negotiation efforts with the rebels, since this confers legitimacy to them. Hence, non-state armed groups can seek to involve mediators because the process itself grants them international legitimacy and recognition (Zartman, 1995).

In addition, a mediator has to gain acceptance from key regional and international actors. A 'patrons-preferred mediator' is a type of mediator that occurs when internal armed conflicts are internationalized and the driving force is the patron's decision to support a particular mediator (Maundi *et al.*, 2006, 25; Mitchell, 1993: 272).

Why Norway in Sri Lanka?

As outlined above, the selection of a particular mediator is dependent on both the demand for, and supply of, mediation. In other words, mediation occurs when there is interest from a mediator to function as a peacemaker, and there simultaneously is an interest from the primary and secondary parties to request third-party mediation from a particular mediator. Consequently, the factors behind the Norwegian mediation effort in Sri Lanka can be sought, not only in the interests of Norway, but also in the availability of other mediators, and the acceptance of Norway by actors related to the conflict.

Norway's interests

Any mediation intervention by Norway has to be understood against the background of peacemaking and reconciliation as one of the cornerstones of Norwegian foreign policy. The peacemaker role is attractive to Norway for several reasons. First of all, Norway is seen as having comparative advantages, and is particularly suited for undertaking mediation activities. Norway has a tradition of solidarity and development assistance dating back to the labour movement; has a relative lack of compromising history; is a rich, resourceful country, and over time has gained knowledge and experience of mediation.

Humanitarian and human rights concerns are also important in this regard.[7]

Secondly, the peacemaking agenda is important for Norway's self-perception. Engaging in peace efforts promotes a national image as a great, moral power. This perception has been cultivated through the many mediation attempts – not only in Sri Lanka, but also in Guatemala, the Middle East and Sudan – that Norway has pursued. 'The country's leaders, supported by a strong public opinion, believe that Norway should actively do what it can to promote international peace' (Kelleher & Taulbee, 2006: 482). The unity around this national image might explain the lack of debate about Norway's international engagement. Its intervention in Sri Lanka is neither a major issue in the domestic political debate, nor in the Norwegian media.[8] Although some academics have recently voiced criticism, generally there has been little interest in the mediation efforts from the Norwegian media.[9]

Thirdly, mediation is important for Norway's international image (Palihapitiya, 2007). Norway has never been a big player in world politics, neither politically nor economically. However, through its peace efforts, Norway has promoted its national interests by gaining a reputation as a skilled and effective peacemaker. The involvement in conflict-torn areas has given it access to the key centres of power in the world, such as the World Bank, and the White House in Washington, D.C. For instance, in the Sri Lankan peace process – particularly during the early stages – the Norwegian mediators

---

7 According to Egeland (1988), Norway and many other smaller Western states have been in a good position to pursue a human rights agenda as part of their foreign policy.

8 The Progress Party (Fremskrittspartiet) has occasionally raised some criticism, but when Norway was attacked in Sri Lanka, it supported Norwegian policy. In recent public debates related to Norway's intervention in Sri Lanka, and elsewhere, see, for instance, Saravanthan and de Soysa (2007); Jagland (2008); Stokke (2008).

9 By contrast, there have been both scholarly and media debates in Sri Lanka on the Norwegian mediation efforts; for instance, Uyangoda (i.e. 2006; 2007b). Also see the debate in *Third World Quarterly* between Saravanthan (2007b) and Stokke (2007).

had access to high-level officials within the US administration. Beyond concerns about a bolstered international image, such positive attention for Norway can have spillover effects that can be positive for public relations, trade relations and other national interests in the longer term. As expressed by Norwegian mediator Erik Solheim: 'the involvement in peace processes creates interest in Norway with other major countries of the world' (Rupesinghe, 2006: 341). From this perspective, Norway's interest in acting as peacemaker in Sri Lanka is not related to the conflict itself, but rather lies in Washington D.C., Brussels and Delhi.

Critics of the Norwegian mediation efforts, mainly based in a Sinhalese Buddhist nationalist ideology, have argued that the main motivations behind its involvement should be sought in Norway's economic interests in Sri Lanka (Wanigasekera, 2008); neo-colonial aspirations (Goonatilake, 2005) and its supposed support to terrorism and the LTTE (Weerasinghe, 2005). This also includes the influence of the Tamil Diaspora in Norway (Rovik, 2005). Due to these motivations, the Norwegian mediation efforts have, according to these critical perspectives, been biased and unbalanced in favour of the LTTE. According to two critics, the 'Norwegians [...] are not, and never have been, a balanced, genuine or honest faciliator' (Gunasekera & Dayasiri, 2006). Yet if one examines these hypotheses, the causal link between these Norwegian interests and its involvement cannot be validated.[10] For instance, although there are common interests in the fishing industry, Sri Lanka is only of marginal importance for Norway's economy and business interests.[11] While the presence of Tamils from Sri Lanka in Norway constituted a link at the outset of the mediation process, this was not the determining factor for Norway's mediation. Representatives of the Diaspora approached Erik Solheim, then a member of the Foreign Policy Committee, as a representative of the Socialist Left Party. At that time, the politi-

---

10 The empirical bearing of these hypotheses is examined in Höglund and Svensson (2008b).

11 According to Erik Solheim, it was also entirely coincidental that Norway was involved in Sri Lanka when natural resources were found (Rupesinghe 2006: 341).

cal spokesperson of the LTTE, Anton Balasingham, was in need of medical treatment, and Solheim took measures to facilitate kidney transplantation in Norway. This connection opened up a direct channel from Norway to the inner circles of the LTTE. However, after this initial contact there has been little direct influence from Tamil Diaspora on the Norwegian mediation efforts.[12] Although there have been some demonstrations and official petitions, the Tamil Diaspora has kept a relatively low political profile. Moreover, there is a perception amongst representatives of the Diaspora in Norway that they have not influenced the Norwegian mediation efforts.[13] However, it has been argued that Norway has been 'misinformed' about existing realities in the war-torn eastern parts of the country because they rely too much on the Diaspora, which is mainly from the north, and are supporters of the LTTE (Saravananthan, 2007a).

Availability and acceptability

One reason why the conflicting parties accepted Norway can be found in the long Norwegian engagement in the development sector. Norway had established ties with Sri Lanka through a series of development projects. The personal contacts and visits in Sri Lanka, through Norwegian Non-Governmental Organisations (NGOs) and individuals (primarily Arne Fjortoft) were crucial in this regard (Martin, 2006).[14]

At the outset of the process, special links were also established that gave Norway access to the inner circles of the LTTE. The Tamil separatist organisation is a strict military and hierarchical organisation without transparency. During the peace process, Norway devel-

---

12 On the Tamil Diaspora in Norway, see e.g. Fuglerud (1999; 2001). Approximately 12,000 Tamils live in Norway (out of a population of 4.6 million people).

13 Confirmed in interviews with members from the Tamil Diaspora in Oslo (February 2008).

14 Fjortoft is a journalist and founder of the Worldview International Foundation (WIF) who has had contacts with Sri Lanka since the 1960s. He has also been the Chairman of the Liberal Party in Norway.

oped into one of the few actors on the international scene that had contacts with, and knowledge about, the LTTE. This gave Norway a quite unique position. The global war against terrorism has had major implications for the potential of peace diplomacy in general, and the question of mediator acceptability in particular. States have been increasingly reluctant to interact with non-state actors who utilize violent means to pursue their political ambitions (Helgesen, 2007; Philipson, 2005). An implication is that it reduces the number of available mediators in conflicts in which one of the parties has been listed as a terrorist entity.

External meditation is particularly sensitive for the government side, since it leaves it vulnerable to the criticism that it is not sufficiently protecting the sovereignty of the state. For this reason, the government of Sri Lanka has been ambivalent to third-party intervention on the island, and has been extremely sensitive to measures that grant recognition to the LTTE. Concern about protecting the sovereignty of Sri Lanka is one factor behind the relative weakness of the United Nations (UN) in Sri Lanka. The UN had a weak position in Sri Lanka throughout the civil war. Its role was mainly limited to humanitarian measures and the protection of displaced civilians (Clarance, 2006). Despite major casualties and human rights abuses from both sides, the UN Security Council has not issued any resolutions on the Sri Lankan conflict.[15]

The acceptance of Norwegian mediation was a question which was also drawn into the internal tension between the major political parties on the Sinhalese side (the UNP and the SLFP) during the time of the peace process. To a large extent, the UNP-led peace process excluded President Kumaratunga (SLFP) from the decision-making process. The President was also increasingly sceptical of Norwegian mediation, although she was the one who originally invited the Norwegians to act as third parties. The election in April 2004, in which the President's party was critical of the Norwegians, brought a SLFP-led coalition back to power.

The acceptance of Norwegian mediation can be seen as a reflec-

---

15 There is only one resolution from the Security Council concerning Sri Lanka – S/RES/109 (1955), dealing with the country's membership of the UN.

tion of a convergence of interest among the primary parties. As a non-state actor with an aspiration of representing a nation, and a nation-state in making, the LTTE has sought recognition and international legitimacy. This factored into its decision to accept a state as mediator. Seen from this perspective, fewer official actors in the field of conflict resolution, such as various NGOs, were probably not acceptable to the LTTE. In addition, more high-stake involvement, such as by the UN, would be unacceptable for the government side. Hence Norway turned out to be a middle-range candidate deemed acceptable by both sides.

Yet there could have been less peaceful motivations from both sides behind accepting an international mediator, and initiating a peace process. In hindsight, it is evident that both sides used the ceasefire to re-arm and re-build their military capacity. Although this was not necessarily the main reason why the parties accepted mediation, it is impossible to exclude the possibility that the perceived benefit of a pause in fighting to re-build strength was one of the motivations behind the ceasefire.

It would not be possible to understand why the task of mediating in Sri Lanka fell on Norway without taking the international and regional context into account. India has a special interest in Sri Lanka due to its role as a regional, great power, and its links to the conflict itself. India has a large Tamil population in Tamil Nadu and supported the Tamil militant groups during the initial years of the Tamil struggle. India has been the most important external actor in the conflict, bringing about the Indo-Lanka Accord of 1987. Yet India burned its fingers when the Indian Peacekeeping Force clashed with the LTTE following the Indo-Lanka Accord, escalating into an open armed conflict. Bearing this traumatic experience in mind, India has been reluctant to be directly involved as a mediator in the conflict.[16] In 1991, Indian Prime Minister, Rajiv Gandhi was assassinated by the LTTE, which excluded official support to them for the foreseeable future.

For a small country like Norway, it is important to be on good footing with this emerging economic great power. India has be-

---

16 On India's intervention, see Bose (2002); Gooneratne (2000); Wriggins (1995).

come a high-priority trade partner for Norway. From 2002, trade with India has increased by 120%.[17] Norway's involvement in Sri Lanka resulted in frequent top-level consultations with India. As a regional, major power player, India has held a de facto veto on the involvement of external third parties into their sphere of influence. Without Indian consent, Norway would not have been given a mandate to negotiate (Keethaponcalan, 2005). It is also generally acknowledged that any solution to the Sri Lankan conflict has to be endorsed by India if it is to be successful.

Sri Lanka is not of major interest for other actors in the international system.[18] Although the US had some strategic interest in gaining access to marine bases in the eastern part of the island, these bases are neither crucial nor the only ones in the region the US has access to. Following 9/11, one of its top priorities has been to curb the international network of financing for terrorists and non-state armed groups. The Sri Lankan conflict has therefore partially been seen through the lens of the international campaign against terrorism. Yet although the US has given military support to the government side, it has maintained the position that a political solution, including substantial devolution of power, is needed for the conflict to be settled (Lunstead, 2007). In line with this, the US has also supported the Norwegian mediation effort. The EU has also supported the Norwegian-led peace process, but following its legal

---

17 In addition, from 2005 to 2006, Norway's export to India increased by 9%, and India's export to Norway increased by 66% (Norwegian Government 2008).

18 The conflict is now increasingly affected by the regional power dynamics, with external powers seeking to increase their own, and counter the influence of others. India is the most important foreign supporter of Sri Lanka, and remains its largest trading partner and supplier of military equipment. Strategically, it is in India's interest to keep its rival China out of its main sphere of influence. China is currently one of Sri Lanka's major military suppliers, but also has a potential for economic investments and infrastructure projects. Likewise, Pakistan's engagement in Sri Lanka is strategically sensitive for India. Sri Lanka, under President Rajapakse, has established closer contacts with Iran. See International Crisis Group (2008) and 'India and China vie for Regional Supremacy' in *Jane's Intelligence Review*, July 1, 2005.

banning of the LTTE in 2006 – a measure which was one of the reasons why the LTTE lost confidence in the peace process – the EU has been seen as too partial to play a constructive role. Similar to Norway, Japan has, to some extent, an ambition to play a peace-enhancing role in the international system. Therefore, Japan has a basic rationale for involvement in Sri Lanka, progressively increased its role in the peace process, and functioned as a constructive complement and supporter of the Norwegian mediation efforts. Since Japan has religious and historical ties to the Sinhalese in Sri Lanka, it has maintained a close relationship with the state, and has less established connections with the LTTE.[19]

The interest behind Norway's mediation effort has also influenced perceptions about bias. Norway was selected as a mediator because the parties saw it as an unbiased intermediary, which had the potential to gain access to both sides. Still, the question of mediation bias has been commonly aired in Sri Lanka. There are, as discussed above, a number of hypotheses about the basis for the Norwegian involvement, and these have also influenced the perception of Norway as being source biased. We have discussed the question of the Norwegian Tamil Diaspora. It is also a commonly held perception within the Sinhalese political discourse that Norway's policy on terrorism has guided and influenced its decision to mediate in Sri Lanka. According to this perspective, Norway is too lax on terrorism and holds a general sympathetic attitude towards non-state actors using armed means to pursue political aims. Norway is seen as a safe haven for terrorists from different parts of the world. This is due to its liberal policies and history of being restrictive in extraditing alleged terrorists. Critics also point to the fact that official LTTE-representatives have acted openly in Norway.[20] Some critics even see Norway as an active supporter of the LTTE, by giving direct and indirect support to the organisation. Norway intervened, according to this perspective, as a strategy of supporting an ally; by offering

---

19 On Japan's role in the peace process, see Perera (2004) and International Crisis Group (2008).

20 See, for instance, Rovik (2005); Goonatilake (2005), and Weerasinghe (2005).

to mediate with LTTE, it gave it an aura of official recognition and statesmanship. The 'black-guarding of Norwegians', in particular in its efforts to treat both parties as equal negotiating partners, is one facet of the extremist Sinhalese Buddhist nationalist ideology (De-Votta, 2007: 33). During, and after the peace process, the Sinhalese nationalist forces grew in strength and influence (Uyangoda, 2007a: 44). These forces have been at the forefront, utilising their influence over the media and political discourse in the south. They have been picturing the Norwegian mediators as foreign intruders, biased in favour of the LTTE-side. Yet the idea that Norway is predisposed to be sympathetic to the LTTE disregards the fact that it has a long history of involvement in aid, trade and diplomatic relations with the government of Sri Lanka. In some respect, Norway could be seen as a country that is generally sympathetic to the Sri Lankan state since it lacks a history of colonialism and has supported the decolonisation processes on a global scale (Egeland, 1988).[21]

Furthermore, the difference in policy towards non-state actors that use violent means is not necessarily a reflection of difference in normative goals between Norway and other democracies. Rather, it could reflect a separation of roles, and Norway's propensity to act as an intermediary in internal armed conflicts around the globe, where too harsh an anti-terrorism legislation would hinder its possibilities to communicate with non-state actors.

The mediation approach and its implications for the negotiation process

How did Norway – its rationale for being involved and its mediation approach – influence the mediation effort in Sri Lanka? The choice of mediator is likely to have implications for both the negotiation process – for instance, how the negotiation process is organised and carried out – and its outcome, including the reasons for its break-down. The Sri Lankan peace process came to a clear endpoint in

---

21 Note that this stands in contrast to the perception in the Sinhalese na-tionalist political discourse, where Norway is seen as having a hidden neo-colonial agenda.

2008, when the government formally withdrew from the ceasefire. However, the negotiations had been stalled since 2003 when the LTTE withdrew from the peace talks. The security situation dramatically deteriorated during 2005 until the war restarted. While the primary reason for the collapse of the peace process relates to the parties' inability to compromise, it is important to evaluate the role of Norway in this regard. The Norwegian mediation approach is organised along three dimensions; namely ownership, impartiality and internationalisation.

Ownership

The Norwegian model of peacemaking has emphasized the parties' ownership of the peace process, where the responsibility, both for the process' design and for its continuation, rests with the parties themselves (Martin, 2006: 125). Consequently, one of the characteristics of the Norwegian mediation approach has been the fact that it builds on the premise that the two major actors in the conflict own the process, and that the external facilitator only plays a consultative role in arranging dialogue. The idea of the primacy of ownership permeates the entire process, and is also an explanation for both the intervention's strength and limitations.

This 'two-party model' – where the sole responsibility for the process lies with the government and the LTTE – has been criticised because it excludes large segments of the Sri Lankan society. Important stakeholders, such as the Muslim minority, non-LTTE Tamil groups, and representatives of civil society, have been left out (Keenan, 2008: 93–94).[22] From the LTTE's perspective, it would be detrimental to their bargaining position if the Muslims were included as an independent actor in the negotiation process. The inclusion of a separate Muslim delegation would weaken the LTTE's claim to represent the

---

22 Although the leader of Sri Lanka Muslim Congress (SLMC), Rauf Hakeem, attended the talks as a member of the Sri Lankan Government delegation, the Muslim minority was never included as an equal independent party to the peace process, which created substantial grievance among the Muslim community (McGilvray and Raheem, 2007; see also Uyangoda, 2007a).

entire north-east of the country. Instead, the LTTE seemed to favour a phased negotiation process, where an agreement between the
government and themselves would then be followed by subsequent
negotiations and agreements between them, and representatives of
the Muslims (Uyangoda, 2007a: 30–31). A consequence of LTTE's
position as the sole representative of the Tamils is that there is little
tolerance for divergent opinions among them in Sri Lanka. Indeed,
the long struggle has made them a highly authoritarian organisation
(Uyangoda, 2007a: 14). Building on the 'two-party model' implied
that other Tamil political organisations had no influence over the
peace process. This type of process is also more vulnerable in times
of crisis because it basically leaves the two major actors in charge of
taking initiatives towards accommodation. Yet the 'two-party model'
also has the advantage of giving the major parties a clear responsibility
for the management and outcome of the process. In this sense, the
mediators were able to get the parties to agree on a ceasefire, which,
at the time, was in the interest of both the parties, but they did not
have the leverage to push the parties to bring political negotiations
to conclusion with an agreement. Without force and pressure, any
agreement reached through this type of process is voluntary, with a
high degree of autonomy for the parties.

Building the peace process on exclusive dialogue between the
two major belligerents has also been a way to manage the potential dilemma between efficiency and legitimacy, by giving primacy
to the former rather than the latter (Belloni, 2008). The ceasefire
agreement (CFA) was reached in a relatively short amount of time.[23]
For the two main parties it was a clear advantage that the design of
the peace process was exclusive in nature.[24] This exclusive character

---

23 It has been argued that the agreement was reached without enough delib-
erations and discussions (Gooneratne, 2007).

24 One of the reasons why the process was exclusively focusing on the two
parties might have been a phased conceptualisation of the peace process: it is
not uncommon that peace processes are elite-driven in the beginning, while
masses are included at a later stage. In Sri Lanka, anchoring the peace process
in the society, and building support and legitimacy among other stakeholders,
were efforts that – given that the peace negotiations would have succeeded –
could have been implemented later in the process.

was one of the reasons why the process was able to move forward with such speed in the beginning. With a more inclusive approach, the peace negotiations would have been less flexible and efficient. However, the 'two-party model', with the two main parties 'owning' the process, ultimately led to reduced legitimacy.

Hence, once the process entered troubled waters, the Norwegians had little possibility to prevent further escalation. In essence, Norway had no power outside the process. The basis for the involvement was the invitation, mandate and continued consent of the two major parties. The Norwegian mediation effort was not based on a resolution from the UN, or a mandate from other regional or global organisations. The only source of leverage that Norway could use over the parties had been within the process. Dialogue, persuasion, and information were tactics that are useful in good times, but less effective in times of escalation. Indeed, the LTTE seemed to realize that, as a mediator, Norway had quite limited leverage: '[f]rom the LTTE's perspective, Norway has not been able to ensure that the Sri Lankan government implemented promises made at negotiations' (Uyangoda, 2006: 6).

Impartiality

The Norwegian approach to peacemaking is, on a general level, characterised by impartiality, confidentiality and consistency, in combination with relatively generous economic resources for developmental assistance (Lieberfeld, 1995). Norway was selected due to its potential to have contact with both sides. During the process, Norway was one of the few actors in the international system that had knowledge and contacts with the LTTE. Indeed, the special link that was established early on between the Norwegians and the LTTE, and over time even developed into personal friendship for the mediator, Erik Solheim (Martin, 2006: 106), may have influenced the perception of bias among some segments of the Sinhalese population. Yet the fact that so few official representatives of organisations or states, except the Norwegians, hold official contacts with the leadership of the LTTE created an image problem for Norway. A large section of the Sri Lankan population, notably within the majority Sinhalese population, saw Norway as favouring the Tamil cause.[25] There could be different reasons for why this perception of mediation bias is so widespread (Höglund & Svensson, 2008a). Yet one of those reasons is precisely because the Norwegian officials were among the few who were publicly in contact with the LTTE.

Norway acted as an impartial mediator. However, impartiality does not necessarily imply complete neutrality. Any mediators carry with them a set of normative values that they can use to influence the way the process is managed. Touval and Zartman posit that 'mediators are seldom indifferent to the terms being negotiated' (Touval & Zartman, 2001: 428). Only on a few occasions have Norway's political and moral positions influenced the content of negotiation and the issues subject to negotiation. One issue where humanitarian concerns overrode the parties' ownership of the process is related to the issue of recruitment of child soldiers. In response to growing local and international criticism, this issue was discussed during the fifth round of peace talks (Human Rights Watch 2004). However, Norway's influence seems to have been only marginal and, for instance, the NGO University Teachers for Human Rights (Jaffna) was outspoken in its criticism of Norway in this regard.

The impartial approach of the Norwegians has been criticised, in particular in light of the asymmetrical degree of violations of the ceasefire agreement. During the ceasefire, the LTTE committed most of the violations (Keenan, 2008: 97). Keenan suggests (2008: 95) that there was a perception among many international and civil society organisations during the ceasefire period that to single out the Tigers for these violations would risk destabilising the peace process. Yet Keenan argues that neglecting to criticise the LTTE for its behaviour and trying to act in a manner of 'evenhandedness' by the Norwegians and other international actors was basically detrimental to the long-term sustainability of the peace process (Keenan, 2008).

During the peace process, one of the most controversial issues was the question of parity between the parties. By treating the two

---

25 See, for instance, the results from the Peace Confidence Index, March 2005. Reports from the survey are published regularly on the website of the Centre for Policy Alternatives (www.cpalanka.org).

sides, although legally asymmetrical, in an equal manner, Norway's mediation style influenced the perception among the government's constituency that Norway was biased in favour of the LTTE (Höglund & Svensson, 2008a). In line with this, Keenan (2008: 100) argues that interventions will in principle always have an effect on the balance between the parties – either in terms of material power or in terms of recognition and other forms of symbolic power. Thus, engaging with official representatives from Norway was an important part of the international recognition sought by the LTTE.

Another characteristic of the Norwegian mediation effort – with implications for the negotiation process – is that it was built on the consent of the regional great power, India. For instance, India's influence was important in determining the composition of the SLMM. While Norway wanted a monitoring mechanism independent from it, neither the Sri Lankan government nor India would accept the involvement of great powers, or the UN. By composing the monitoring mission from observers exclusively from Nordic countries, including Norway, this created an awkward situation in that Norway was acting as both a mediator and an observer of the peace-process implementation. This dual role also had implications for the perception about third-party bias, since many people in Sri Lankan did not recognise that the SLMM was separate from the mediation effort.

Internationalisation

The peace process in Sri Lanka has been dominated by a high degree of internationalisation. Norway has been instrumental in the efforts to direct the attention and wider engagement of the international community towards Sri Lanka. Norway's interest in cultivating its international reputation as a peacemaker explains its interest to get involved. It also explains its interest, once it was involved, in putting this conflict on the radar screen of the international community. We have argued that Norway's interest in acting as a peacemaker in Sri Lanka was related to its aspiration to be a significant voice in the international system. Yet the internationalisation of the peace process backfired. The high involvement of the international community provoked mistrust on the part of the LTTE about the entire process. A trend in the international community has been a lowered tolerance for the LTTE. When more countries listed the LTTE as a terrorist organisation – Canada and the EU in 2006, the United Kingdom in 2001, and so on – the LTTE grew more frustrated. The possibility for Norway to convince them about the viability of peace talks waned. It also limited the possibility for Norway to persuade the LTTE of finding alternative visions to address the underlying Tamil grievance.

In many ways, Norway was dependent on leverage from other countries. Yet declarations of the need for both sides to respect the ceasefire, promises of economic assistance, and threats to ban the LTTE, were efforts by other countries that, in the end, were not enough to get the parties back to the negotiation table (Goodhand & Klem, 2005).

The international campaign against terrorism had, as discussed earlier, implications for the selection of mediators. Yet it also had implications for how the peace process unfolded. For instance, one of the explicit reasons for the withdrawal of the Tamil Tigers from the peace talks was their exclusion from a preparatory meeting held in Washington in April 2003, ahead of a major donor conference in Tokyo (Balasingham, 2004: 430). The US listing of the LTTE was a legal obstacle for their inclusion in this meeting. Hence, the terrorism prism through which the US viewed the conflict turned out to be unproductive for the continuation of the peace process. Likewise, the decision of the EU to put the LTTE on their list of banned organisations, after pressure from the US, substantially de-creased the possibility for the EU to act constructively in the conflict (Lunstead, 2007). Drawn into the dynamics of the international campaign against terrorism, the power relations between the two contestants were affected. The expectation of the government that they could defeat the LTTE through military means, rather than reaching an agreement at the negotiation table, increased.

The peace process was, as discussed above, characterised by relatively high degrees of both ownership and internationalisation. Yet there is also a tension between these two traits: a more interna-tionalised process can lead to a reduced sense of ownership for the parties. This was a line of criticism from the LTTE, which left the talks in protest against 'excessive involvement' by the international actors (Balasingham, 2004: 434). But the tension between these two characteristics also played out in the other direction in the Sri Lankan case: the ownership of the process reduced the level of internationalisation. Since the two main parties 'owned' the process, the international community had little possibility to exert influence on them in matters that were seen as important for the international community, such as respect for human rights, protection of civilians, and a negotiated settlement of the conflict.

Conclusion

The civil war in Sri Lanka has shown itself remarkably resistant to resolution. The return to the battlefield after six years of first an actual, and then a nominal, ceasefire between the government and the LTTE marked an endpoint to the peace process. To give a definitive assessment of the success or failure of the Norwegian intervention is much too early at this stage. The ceasefire agreement, by implementing a lull in the fighting, saved a substantial number of lives. Also, during the period it was respected, it significantly and positively affected the living conditions for all civilians on the island. Moreover, the efforts by the Norwegian mediators could very well have laid the ground for future dialogue and solutions. Yet the third-party intervention was also a failure. Our analysis identifies some points that need to be taken into account in the debate on this issue.

A number of factors have driven the Norwegian engagement in Sri Lanka. These can be found at three different levels: the readiness of the mediator; the acceptance of the primary parties, and the consent of the regional and global powers. As argued above, the ambition of Norway to function as a peacemaker in the international system was one of the driving forces behind its willingness to act as a mediator in this conflict. The acceptance of the parties has to do with access, international recognition, and impartiality. The consent of India and the US to accept Norwegian peacemaking is found in an interest in keeping outside Sri Lanka other, more influential, actors with more direct interests.

The Norwegian mediation revealed a weakness of the ownership approach to the process. Even if the approach is appealing in theory, it carries difficulties in practice. It puts the responsibility of the process entirely on the antagonists, who can face problems to level themselves above escalatory dynamics. At the same time, the primacy of ownership is a reflection of a situation on the ground, where the two major armed parties, the government and the LTTE, had the veto-power over the design of the process, which a mediator without authority, such as Norway, has really little influence over.

The Norwegian approach to mediation was also built on impartiality. However, it was difficult to uphold the image of impartiality in the asymmetrical setting of the Sri Lankan conflict. The complexity created by the fact that Norway played multiple roles – taking a lead role in the monitoring mission, while at the same time facilitating the peace talks – also factored into the perceptions of bias.

We have suggested that the regional and global power-dynamics created the particular context that made Norwegian mediation possible, but also undermined its possibility of success. The international community, by failing to convince the parties with the carrots of aid and financial support, or the sticks involving terrorist listing, was not effective in pushing or pulling the parties towards peace. Yet it is important that actors like Norway exist in the international context and can function as channels of communication with non-state actors, who continue to be part of the international system. With the international war on terror, there are fewer mediators that are available to play this peacemaking role.

At the same time, it is important to bear in mind that the Sri Lankan conflict has shown itself remarkably resistant to conflict resolution efforts, including international mediation. Ultimately, mediation and negotiation proved to be important, but insufficient, instruments for dealing with the state-formation conflict in Sri Lanka. Although they were fruitful in getting the process initiated, mediation and negotiation failed to address the basic underlying question of different forms of nationalism competing for state power. Moreover, the peace mediation in Sri Lanka did not succeed in addressing the obstacles for a peaceful solution, and in some aspects added to the intractability of the conflict. In this respect, mediation is a risky endeavour.

Changing Roles and Practices

Karin Aggestam & Annika Björkdahl

Introduction

To manage conflict dynamics and strengthen peace processes is an enormous challenge to the external actors concerned. A key question pertains to the timing of interventions by outside actors. At what point should international actors become involved in a conflict? An obvious problem is whether or not to respond to calls for attention and swift action from conflict-ridden societies. At the same time, lack of political will has become a major stumbling-block in the mobilisation of resources and personnel for peace-support operations. The reasons and motivations of external actors vary and influence the extent of their engagement.

The motivation and timing of entry into a conflict will consequently determine the strategies and tools used by the external actors. The international community has a vast range of approaches, strategies and instruments in its toolbox to build peace. Yet how to combine peacemaking strategies in the most efficient way is still unresolved. Different strategies are frequently implemented simultaneously, but without serious consideration of whether the strategies reinforce or undermine each other.

This points to the challenge of coordination and cooperation between the multitude of external actors on the ground in order to avoid unnecessary overlaps and to establish some kind of division of labour. However, it is necessary to strike a balance between the responsibilities of local and external actors. Peace can only be achieved through a combination of activities undertaken by local and external actors in order to be sustainable also when the external actors withdraw. This points to the common critique that external actors do too little, too late and leave too early. When and how should external actors disengage and transfer responsibility to the local actors? The problem of exit affects decisions concerning entry, since a pre-determined exit date and a prepared exit strategy are sometimes preconditions for engagement.

Challenges of entry

The literature on escalation models of violent conflicts provides important insights about the appropriate timing to initiate conflict prevention, management and resolution (see for example, Zartman & Faure, 2005). Concepts such as early warning, preventive diplomacy and preventive action indicate that external actors should undertake actions early in the conflict cycle prior to the outbreak of systematic violence. In the early phase of the conflict, levels of hostilities are low, casualties are generally few, memories of atrocities are limited and this in turn may serve to make peace more likely (Lund, 1996). In contrast, Stedman argues that preventive diplomacy provides no easy solution and should not be oversold. Despite the attractiveness of the notion of prevention, an international political will needs to be mobilised, interests and motives must be spelled out, priorities set and scarce resources balanced (Stedman, 1995).

Another frequently used notion of timing is the 'ripeness' of conflict; that is, a mutually hurting stalemate (Zartman, 1989) or an enticing opportunity (Mitchell, 1995). Birger Heldt explores in his chapter the timing of intervention by external actors in recently initiated, low-level intrastate conflicts. The findings presented suggest that disputants in the early phase of an escalating conflict should avoid unaided, direct face-to-face talks, and preferably communicate indirectly through a third-party.

Höglund and Svensson also address the problematique of the appropriate timing of mediation efforts. The involvement of external actors, in this case the mediation of Norway in the Sri Lankan peace process, is a function of supply and demand for mediation. In other words, 'the mediation will occur when there is interest from a mediator to function as a peacemaker, and simultaneously there is an interest from the primary and secondary parties to request third-party mediation from a particular mediator' as argued by Höglund and Svensson in this volume. Highlighting the demand for external engagement from the parties to the conflict leads to the important issue of consent. In contemporary international relations, sovereignty is still the overriding principle guiding state interaction. Like any norm, sovereignty changes over time, but most external actors still respect the norm and avoid intervening in the internal affairs of other states (Björkdahl, 2006: 214–228). Hence, for external actors to attempt to manage conflicts within states and promote peacebuilding, consent remains a key aspect. In internal conflicts such as the one between the government of Sri Lanka and the Liberation Tigers of Tamil Eelam (LTTE), the government position is more powerful in terms of legitimacy and international recognition, which is a common characteristic of contemporary asymmetrical conflicts.

Consenting to third-party mediation in negotiations with separatists, may somewhat alter the balance or power, as it confers legitimacy to the non-state actor as well as some type of international recognition. Consent by the host country has traditionally been one of the main principles of peacekeeping and regarded as crucial for both deployment and success. In contemporary peace operations, where the use of force or the threat of use of force is a viable option, the issue of consent is increasingly complex, as Kersti Larsdotter argues in her chapter. It is not only important to gain consent from the political elite of the main parties to the conflict, that is, at the military strategic level, but also to gain consent at the tactical level, which refers to the will of the local population.

A prerequisite for outside involvement is the ability to muster a political will among the key members of the international society to take swift and resolute action in times of crisis. Maria Småberg illustrates in her chapter that the lack of political will is not only a contemporary phenomenon due to humanitarian fatigue. The lack of international response to the early-warning signals from, among others, the Swedish missionary who witnessed the onset of the genocide of the Armenians clearly demonstrates the limited interest of the great powers in the early 20th century in reacting to, and alleviating, the suffering of a small nation.

Challenges midway

A basic challenge for outside actors pertains to cooperation and coordination and whether to engage in top-down or bottom-up policies: to establish, reform and strengthen democratic institutions; to persuade and coerce war-makers to abstain from violence and negotiate with political leaders, or to foster a functioning civil society in the hope that strong peace constituencies will influence the political elite and cultivate self-sustainable peace in the long term. Maria Småberg highlights the bottom-up approach in her analysis of the female missionary and peacebuilder at the local level, supporting the civil society through health work rather than spreading Christianity to the local community. A justifiable criticism of the top-down approach is that it is not founded in or adapted to the local context (Chopra, 2002). This in turn creates a sense of lack of ownership of the peace efforts and peacebuilding processes among the local population in war-torn societies. Michael Schulz underlines in his chapter the importance of a multitrack approach to peacebuilding as a means of including the broader civil society and to ensure local ownership and needs, interests and visions of peace. The difficulty of allowing for local ownership is revealed in the Norwegian mediation in Sri Lanka, where both the antagonists held veto-powers over the outcome of the mediation process, rendering the mediator powerless to push for a specific outcome.

The interaction between international and local actors is dynamic and complicated, yet crucial for the successful transition from war to peace. Kersti Larsdotter provides insights into the dynamics of interaction between international and local actors in Afghanistan. Peacekeepers in contemporary complex, multi-dimensional, hybrid missions will often be in close interaction with the local population, and ensuring their collaboration and understanding is deemed to be essential to the success of the operation. The ability of ISAF-peacekeepers to use force affects the interaction with the local Afghan population. Larsdotter illustrates that under such circumstances minimum use of force or use of force in protection of the local population may contribute to strengthening the relationship between the outside and the inside actors. The experience of the British-led Provisional Reconstruction Teams (PRTs) demonstrated the efficiency of minimum use of force, which gained the acceptance of the parties as well as the local population. In contrast, the German-led PRTs' approach to the use of force at the tactical level could better be described as 'show of force', with large number of troops wearing body armour on patrolling missions, travelling in heavily protected vehicles, and inclined to more robust use of force.

Cooperation and coordination between state and non-state actors is a contentious issue in the field of security, which raises questions about the division of labour between public and private security actors and about state control and monopoly of violence. The growth of private military and security companies (PMSCs), active in the midst of conflict or in post-conflict settings, contributes to the general trend of privatisation of war and peace. According to Anna Leander, this trend can be traced to contemporary neoliberal practices, which makes the question of accountability of these actors particularly troublesome. Moreover, there are divergent views on what kind of actions should be taken to improve international regulation of PMSCs. As argued by Joakim Berndtsson, the increase in the number of PMSCs changes the composition of the instruments of force and with it the basis of state control, thereby challenging the functional, political control, as well as the social control central to civil-military relations. The extent of security privatisation in Iraq is unparalleled, with PMSCs providing a number of both civilian and military functions, such as training, SSR, armed-convoy escort services, translators, bodyguards for NGOs, states and their armed forces. Most PMSCs in Iraq operate outside the traditional military chain of command, which creates additional problems of collaboration and coordination.

Closely related to collaboration and coordination is the key challenge of how to sequence the numerous activities undertaken by the myriad of actors engaged in a particular conflict setting. As Birger Held demonstrates, if peace talks are properly sequenced, synergies between various peace-promoting activities can be found and the cumulative effect achieved will be more advantageous. However, several peace processes often lack coordination and collaboration between various peacemakers, which may generate counterproductive results.

Challenges of exit

There are several conflicts, such as the asymmetrical conflict in Sri Lanka, which may be described as intractable because they prove to be remarkably resistant to resolution. This makes the exit of external actors particularly challenging. As already mentioned, many peace-support operations and peacebuilding missions are conditioned by the existence of a pre-planned exit strategy. The result of such a precondition may be a premature withdrawal of troops, resources and overall engagement before a situation of self-sustainable peace has been established. The holding of elections is a preferred strategy to boost the legitimacy of a peace accord. It is also a common exit strategy, which characterised several of the 1990s peace-support operations. Early elections have also been used to transfer authority and responsibility from international actors to newly-elected political elites. This has been perceived as a swift way of withdrawing, while at the same time countering criticism of lack of local ownership and accusations of neo-imperialism and neo-colonialism. Yet as Roland Paris (2004) underlines, there are great risks in holding premature elections in vulnerable post-conflict societies, as they tend to generate counterproductive results, such as ethnically based party systems, polarisation of the electorate, and large-scale violence. They risk sparking violence during the campaigning and the elections themselves, and after the results are out (Höglund 2008). Voters in Bosnia-Herzegovina, for example, believed that they had to counterbalance the expected nationalistic voting of the other ethnic groups and felt compelled to vote for their ethnic-based parties. Also, even though electoral contest is obviously to be preferred to violent contest, militants transformed into politicians tend to continue the conflict by other means.

Continued international presence to monitor implementation

of peace accords has proved central to the establishment of a self-sustainable peace. International NGOs may also be able to continue monitoring and assisting a development towards self-sustainable peace and to collaborate with and support local NGOs and representatives of the civil society. In general terms, the existence of vibrant civic organisations can counter the top-down tendencies of the political elites and international regulations and provide local participation and ownership to the peace process. Due to the legacy of the conflicts, most post-war civil societies are likely to be dominated by sectarian groups. However, some groups strive to promote 'civic politics' in contrast to ethnic politics and to open up a political space to articulate local ideas of peace (Belloni, 2008). These groups may therefore function as pro-peace constituencies and be central to the self-sustainability of peace.

In conclusion, external actors face a number of challenges, where the choice of timing is deemed essential for successful and efficient third-party intervention. Another critical aspect is the challenging task of coordination and cooperation, due to the multitude of actors who are engaged in contemporary peace-support operations.

References

Abadi, Jacob, 2001. 'Sweden's policy toward Israel: constraints and adjustments', *Middle Eastern Studies* 37 (2), pp. 23–49.

Abrahamsen, Rita & Michael C. Williams, 2006a. *The Globalization of Private Security: Country Report Nigeria.* Aberystwyth: University of Wales, available at: http://users.aber.ac.uk/rbh/privatesecurity/publications.html.

–, 2006b. *The Globalization of Private Security: Country Report Sierra Leone.* Aberystwyth: University of Wales, available at: http://users.aber.ac.uk/rbh/privatesecurity/publications.html.

–, 2007. 'Introduction: The Privatisation and Globalisation of Security in Africa', *International Relations* 21(2), pp.131–141.

Abu-Nimer, Mohammed, 1999. *Dialogue, Conflict Resolution, and Change: Arab-Jewish Encounters in Israel.* Albany, N.Y.: State University of New York Press.

Ackerman, Alice, 2003. 'The Idea and Practice of Conflict Prevention', *Journal of Peace Research* 40(3), pp. 339–347.

Aftenposten, 2004. 'Parliament in Uproar Over Soldiers Shooting Dogs', *Aftenposten*, 20 February, available at: <http://www.aftenposten.no/english/local/article736190.ece?service=print, last accessed 16 December 2008.

Aggestam, Karin, 2002. 'Mediating Asymmetrical Conflict', *Mediterranean Politics* 7 (1), pp. 69–91.

–, (ed.), 2004. *(O)rättfärdiga Krig.* Lund: Studentlitteratur.

–, & Christer Jönsson, 1997. '(Un)Ending Conflict: Challenges in Post-War Bargaining.' *Millennium: Journal of International Studies* 26(3), pp. 771–793.

Alexander, Klinton W., 2000. 'NATO's intervention in Kosovo: The legal case for violating Yugoslavia's "National Sovereignty", in the absence of Security Council approval', *Houston Journal of International Law* 22 (3), pp. 1–41.

Andersson, Irene, 2001. *Kvinnor mot krig. Aktioner och nätverk för fred 1914–1940.* Lund: Lund University.

Angstrom, Jan & Isabelle Duyvesteyn (eds.), 2007. *Understanding Victory and Defeat in Contemporary War.* London: Routledge.

Anonymous 01, interviewed in 2005.

Anonymous 02, interviewed in 2005.

Aoun, Elena, 2003. 'European Foreign policy and the Arab-Israeli Dispute: Much Ado About Nothing?', *European Foreign Affairs Review* 8(3), pp. 289–312.

Arsdale, van, Lee, Col. (Retd), Chief Executive Officer, Triple Canopy. Interviewed in Washington D.C., May 10, 2007.

Arreguín-Toft, Ivan, 2007. 'How to Lose a War on Terror: A Comparative Analysis of a Counterinsurgency Success and Failure', in Jan Angstrom and Isabelle Duyvesteyn (eds.), *Understanding Victory and Defeat in Contemporary War*. London: Routledge, pp. 142–167.

Atieh, Adel, Gilad Ben-Nun, Gasser El Shahed, Rana Taha & Steve Tulliu, 2005. *Peace in the Middle East. P2P and the Israeli-Palestinian Conflict*, Geneva: UNIDIR/2004/33, United Nations.

Avant, Deborah, 2004. 'The Privatization of Security and Change in the Control of Force', *International Studies Perspectives* 5(2), pp. 153–157.

–, 2005. *The Market for Force: The Consequences of Privatizing Security.* Cambridge: Cambridge University Press.

Bailes, Alison & Caroline Holmqvist, 2007. *The Increasing Role of Private Military and Security Companies*, available at: http://www.isis-europe.org/pdf/2008–artrel–145–07-10-epstudy-pmc&psc.pdf.

Balasingham, Anton. 2004. *War and Peace: Armed Struggle and Peace Efforts of Liberation Tigers.* Mitcham: Fairmax Publishing.

BBC News, 2007: 'Iraqis Angry at Blackwater Shooting' of September 19, available at: http://news.bbc.co.uk/2/hi/middle–east/7003473.stm, accessed September 24, 2008.

Bar-Tal, Daniel, 2001. 'Why Does Fear Override Hope in Societies Engulfed by Intractable Conflict, as It Does in the Israeli Society?' *Political Psychology* 22, (3).

Bearpark, Andy & Sabrina Schulz, 2007. 'The future of the market', in Simon Chesterman & Chia Lehnardt (eds.) *From Mercenaries to Market: The Rise and Regulation of Private Military Companies*. Oxford: Oxford University Press, pp. 239–251.

Beese, C., MBE Chief Administrative Officer, Armor Group, Interviewed July 19, 2006.

Bellamy, Alex J. & Paul Williams, 2004. 'Introduction: Thinking Anew about Peace Operations'. *International Peacekeeping* 11(1), pp. 1–15.

Bellamy, Alex J., Paul Williams & Stuart Griffin, 2004. *Understanding Peacekeeping.* Cambridge: Polity Press.

Belloni, Roberto, 2008. 'Civil Society in War-to-Democracy Transitions', in Anna Jarstad & Timothy D. Sisk (eds.), *From War to Democracy: Dilemmas of Peacebuilding.* Cambridge: Cambridge University Press, pp. 182–210.

Bercovitch, Jacob (ed.), 2002. *Studies in International Mediation.* Basingstoke: Palgrave.

Bercovitch, Jacob & Scott S. Gartner, 2006. 'Is There a Method in the Madness of Mediation: Some Lessons for Mediators from Quantitative Studies of Mediation', *International Interactions* 32(4), pp. 329–354.

Bercovitch, Jacob, Victor Kremenyk & I. William Zartman (eds.), 2008. *Handbook of Conflict Resolution.* Thousand Oaks, CA: Sage Publications.

Bergonzi, Bernard, 1965. *Heroes Twilight: A Study of the Literature of the Great War.* London: CowardMcCann, Inc.

Berman, Sheri, 2007. 'The Sequencing Fallacy', *Journal of Democracy* 18(1), pp. 28–41.

Betts, Wendy, 1999. 'Third Party Mediation: An Obstacle to Peace in Nagorno Karabakh'. *SAIS Review* 19(2), pp. 161–183.

Biddle, Stephen D., 2006. *Military Power: Explaining Victory and Defeat in Modern Battle.* Princeton, N.J.: Princeton University Press.

Bislev, Sven, 2004. 'Privatization of Security as Governance Problem: Gated Communities in the San Diego Region', *Alternatives* 29, pp. 599–618.

Bjork, Kjell & Richard Jones, 2005. 'Overcoming Dilemmas Created by the 21st Century Mercenaries: conceptualising the use of private security companies in Iraq', *Third World Quarterly* 26(4–5), pp. 777–796.

Björkdahl, Annika, 2006. 'Promoting Norms Through Peacekeeping: UN-PREDEP and Conflict Prevention', *International Peacekeeping*13(2), pp. 214–228.

Bjørnlund, Matthias, 2005. 'Ett Folk Myrdes: Det Armeniske Folkmord i Danske Kilder', Master's Thesis, Copenhagen: Copenhagen University.

–, 2006. 'Before the Armenian Genocide: Danish Missionary and Rescue Operations in the Ottoman Empire, 1900–1914', *Haigazian Armenological Review* 26, pp. 141–64.

Bonn International Center for Conversion, 'Security Sector Reform in Afghanistan', available at: http://www.bicc.de/ssr–gtz/pdf/afghanistan.pdf, last accessed 16 December 2008.

Bose, Sumantra, 2002. 'Flawed Mediation, Chaotic Implementation: The 1987 Indo-Sri Lanka Peace Agreement', in J.S Stedman, D. Rothchild & E. M. Cousens (eds.), *Ending Civil Wars: The Implementation of Peace Agreements.* Boulder & London: Lynne Rienner Publishers.

Boulding, Elise, 1976. *The Underside of History: A View of Women through Time.* New York: Halsted.

Brown, Judith M. & Louis, Wm. Roger, (eds.), 1999. *The Oxford History of the British Empire. Volume IV. The Twentieth Century.* Oxford and New York: Oxford University Press.

Carnegie Commission on Preventing Deadly Conflict, 1997. *Preventing Deadly Conflict. Executive Summary of the Final Report.* New York: Carnegie Corporation of New York.

Carothers, Thomas, 2007. 'The Sequencing Fallacy', *Journal of Democracy* 18(1), pp. 12–27.

Chaudhuri, Nupur & Margeret Strobel (eds.), 1992. *Western Women and Imperialism: Complicity and Resistance.* Bloomington: Indiana University Press,

Chesterman, Simon & Chia Lehnardt, 2007. *From Mercenaries to Market: The Rise and Regulation of Private Military Companies.* Oxford: Oxford University Press.

Chin, Warren, 2007. 'Examining the Application of British Counterinsurgency Doctrine by the American Army in Iraq', *Small Wars & Insurgencies* 18(1), pp. 1–26.

Chopra, Jarat, 2002. 'Relief and Reconstruction Building State Failure in East Timor', *Development and Change* 33(5), pp. 979–1000.

Clapham, Christopher, 1996. *Africa and the International System. The Politics of State Survival.* Cambridge: Cambridge University Press.

Clarance, William, 2006. *Ethnic Warfare in Sri Lanka and the U.N. Crisis.* London: Pluto Press.

Cockburn, Cynthia, 2007. *From Where We Stand. War, Women's Activism & Feminist Analysis.* London: Zed Books.

Cohen, William A., 2004. *The Art of the Strategist.* New York: AMACOM.

Coleman, James R., 2004. 'Constraining Modern Mercenarism', *Hastings Law Journal* 55, pp. 1493–1537.

Crescenzi, Mark J. & Andrew J. Enterline, 2001. 'Time Remembered: A Dynamic Model of Interstate Interaction', *International Studies Quarterly* 45(3), pp. 409–431.

Crocker, Chester, Fen Osler Hampson & Pamela Aall (eds.), 2004. *Taming Intractable Conflict: Mediation in the Hardest Cases.* Washington, D.C.: United States Institute for Peace Press.

Dachs & Peters, 2005. 'Israel and Europe, the troubled relationship: between perception and reality'. Paper at the *Centre for the Study of European Politics and Society.*

Darby, John (ed.), 2001. *The Effects of Violence on Peace Processes.* Washington, D.C.: United States Institute of Peace.

–, and Roger MacGinty, (eds.), 2003. *Contemporary Peacemaking. Conflict, Violence and Peace Processes.* Basingstoke and New York: Palgrave Macmillan.

Daniel, Don (ed.), 2008. *Prospects for Peace Operations: Institutional and National Dimensions.* Washington DC.: Georgetown University Press.

De Cuéllar, Javier Perez, 1997. *Pilgrimage for Peace.* New York: St. Martin's.

De Lombaerde, Philippe (ed.), 2006. *Indicators of Regional Integration.* London: Routledge.

Del Sarto, Raffaela A., 2007, 'Wording and Meaning(s): EU-Political Cooperation According to the ENP Action Plan', *Mediterranean Politics* 12 (1), pp. 59–75.

Department of Defense (DOD), October 18, 2007. *DoD News Briefing with Secretary Gates and Adm. Mullen from the Pentagon, Arlington, VA.*, available at: http://www.defenselink.mil/transcripts/transcript.aspx?transcriptid=4064, last accessed March 28, 2008.

DeVotta, Neil, 2007. *Sinhala Buddhist Nationalist Ideology: Implications for Politics and Conflict Resolution in Sri Lanka.* Washington D.C.: East-West Center.

de Wolf, Antenor Hallo, 2007. 'Privatizing War from the Perspective of International and Human Rights Law', *Indiana Journal of Global Legal Studies* 13 (3), pp. 15–35.

Diamond, Louise & John McDonald, 1996. *Multi-Track Diplomacy. A System Approach to Peace.* West Hartford/Connecticut: Kumarian Press.

Dickinson, Laura A., 2007. 'Contracts as a Tool for Regulating PMCs', in Simon Chesterman & Chia Lehnardt (eds.), *From Mercenaries to Market: The Rise and Regulation of Private Military Companies.* Oxford: Oxford University Press, pp. 217–238.

Dieckhoff, Alain, 2005. 'The European Union and the Israeli-Palestinian Conflict', *Journal Inroads* 16, pp. 52–62 (online version).

Diehl, Paul F., 1994. 'What are they Fighting For: The Importance of Issues in International Conflict Research', *Journal of Peace Research* 29(3), pp. 333–344.

Dobbie, Charles, 1994. 'A Concept for Post-Cold War Peacekeeping', *Survival* 36(3), pp. 121–148.

Donald, Dominick, 2006. 'After the Bubble: British Private Security Companies After Iraq', *Whitehall Paper 66*, London: The Royal United Services Institute (RUSI).

Donald, Dominick, Senior Analyst, Aegis Specialist Risk Management. Interviewed in London, May 29, 2007.

Dorn, Nicholas & Michael Levi, 2007a. 'European Private Security, Corporate Investigation and Military Services: Collective Security, Market Regulation and Structuring the Public Sphere', *Policing & Society* 17 (2), pp. 13–38.

–, 2007b. 'Private-Public or Public-Private? Strategic Dialogue on Serious Crime and Terrorism in the EU', *Security Journal*, forthcoming.

Doswald-Beck, Louise, 2007. 'Private Military Companies Under International Humanitarian Law' in Simon Chesterman & Chia Lehnardt (eds.), *From Mercenaries to Markets: The Rise and Regulation of Private Military Companies.* Oxford: Oxford University Press, pp. 115–38.

Doyle, Michael W. & Nicholas Sambanis, 2006. *Making War & Building Peace.* Princeton: Princeton University Press.

Duffield, Mark, 1997. 'NGO Relief in War Zones: Towards an Analysis of the New Aid Paradigm', *Third World Quarterly*, 18 (3), pp. 527–542.

–, 2001. *Global Governance and the New Wars. The Merging of Development and Security.* London and New York: Zed Books.

The Economist, 2003. 'Military-Industrial Complexities', 3/29/2003, 366(8317), pp. 55–56, March 29.

Egeland, Jan, 1988. *Impotent Superpower – Potent Small Power: Potentials and Limitations of Human Rights Objectives in the Foreign Policies of the United States and Norway.* Oslo: Norwegian University Press.

Ekelöf, Gunnar, 1959. *Opus incertum*. Stockholm: Bonniers.

Elsea, Jennifer K. & Nina M. Serafino, 2007. 'CRS [Congerssional Research Service] Report for Congress, July 11, 2007: Private Security Contractors in Iraq: Background, Legal Status, and Other Issues', available at: http://www.fas.org/sgp/crs/natsec/RL32419.pdf, accessed October 26, 2007.

Englund, Peter, 2001. 'Blick och förbländning – om vittneslitteraturens problem och möjligheter', Lecture in Stockholm, 4 December 2001, on a *symposium on witness literature* arranged by the Swedish Academy, available at: http:www.peterenglund.com/textarkiv/blickblandning.htm last accessed 10 April 2007. 10 April 2007.

Etherington, Norman (ed.), 2005. *Missions and Empire*. Oxford and New York: Oxford University Press.

Eurobarometer: www.gesis.org/en/data–service/eurobarometer/standard–eb/index.htm

European Community, *The Venice Declaration*, 1980, available at: http://www. domino.un.org/unispal.NSF/d80185e9f0c69a7b85256cbf005afeac/fef015e8b1a1e5a685256d810059d922.

Evans, Gareth, 2008. *The Responsibility to Protect. Ending Mass Atrocity Crimes Once and for All*. Washington DC.: Brookings Institute.

Falkner, Simon, OBE, Col. (Retd). Interviewed in London, May 30, 2007.

Fearon, James D. & David D. Laitin, 2004. 'Neotrusteeship and the Problem of Weak States', *International Security* 28(4), pp. 5–43.

Feaver, Peter D., 1999. 'Civil-Military Relations', *Annual Review of Political Science* 2, pp. 211–241.

–, 2003. *Armed Servants: Agency, Oversight, and Civil-Military Relations*. Cambridge (Mass.) and London: Harvard University Press.

Feigenbaum, H. *et al.*, 1999. *Shrinking the State: The Political Underpinnings of Privatization*. Cambridge: Cambridge University Press.

Field Manual 3–24, Counterinsurgency, 2006.

Findlay, Trevor, 2002. *The Use of Force in UN Peace Operations*. Oxford: Oxford University Press.

Finer, S. E., 2006 [1962]. *The Man on Horseback: The Role of the Military in Politics*. New Brunswick and London: Transaction Publishers.

Fischer, Ronald J. & Loraleigh Keashly, 1991. 'The Potential Complementarity of Mediation and Consultation within a Contingency Model of Third Party Intervention', *Journal of Peace Research* 28(1), pp. 29–42.

Foreign and Commonwealth Office, Freedom of Information Release, 22 November 2006, 'Private Security Firms in Iraq and Afghanistan', available at: http://www.fco.gov.uk/Files/kfile/PSFs.doc,

Forman, Shepard & Stewart Patrick (eds.), 2000. *Good Intentions. Pledges of Aid for Postconflict Recovery*. Boulder/London: Lynne Rienner Publisher.

Frye, Ellen L., 2005. 'Private Military Firms in the New World Order: How

Redefining "Mercenary" can Tame the "Dogs of War"', *Fordham Law Review* 73(2), pp. 607–664.

Fuglerud, Oivind, 1999. *Life on the Outside: the Tamil Diaspora and Long Distance Nationalism.* London: Pluto Press.

–, 2001. 'Time and Space in the Sri Lanka-Tamil Diaspora', *Nations and Nationalism* 7(2), pp. 195–213.

Gaunt, David, 2006. *Massacres, Resistance, Protectors: Muslim-Christian Relations in Eastern Anatolia During World War I.* Piscataway, NJ: Gorgias Press.

–, 2007. 'Ottoman Bystanders'. *Report for Forum för Levande Historia.* Stockholm: Forum för Levande Historia.

Gerner, Kristian & Klas-Göran Karlsson, 2005. *Folkmordens historia. Perspektiv på det moderna samhällets skuggsida.* Stockholm: Atlantis.

Goertz, Gary & Paul F. Diehl, 1992. *Territorial Changes and International Conflict.* New York N.Y.: Routledge.

Goldman, Anita, 1998. *Snäckans sång. En bok om kvinnor och krig.* Stockholm: Natur och Kultur.

Goldman, Dorothy (ed.), 1993. *Women and World War I: The Written Response.* Basingstoke: Macmillan.

Gomez, Ricardo, 2003. *Negotiating the Euro-Mediterranean Partnership. Strategic Action in EU Foreign Policy?* Aldershot: Ashgate Publishing Limited.

Goodhand, Jonathan, 2006. *Aiding Peace? The Role of NGOs in Armed Conflict.* Boulder/London: Lynne Rienner Publishers.

Goodhand, Jonathan & Bart Kle, 2005. *Aid, Conflict and Peacebuilding in Sri Lanka.* Colombo: The Asia Foundation.

Goonatilake, Susantha, 2005. 'Norway, a 25 Year Odyssey: From Sympathizer to Colonial Intruder', in *Peace in Sri Lanka: Obstacles and Opportunities.* Nugegoda: World Alliance for Peace in Sri Lanka.

Gooneratne, John, 2000. *A Decade of Confrontation: Sri Lanka and India in the 1980s.* Pannipitya: Stamford Lake Publications.

–, 2007. *Negotiating with the Tigers (LTTE) (2002–2005): A View from the Second Row.* Pannipitiya: Stamford Lake Publications.

Government Accountability Office (GAO), July 2005: 'Rebuilding Iraq: Actions Needed to Improve Use of Private Security Providers', available at: http://www.gao.gov/highlights/d05737high.pdf, accessed March 27, 2008.

–, June 2006. 'Rebuilding Iraq: Actions Still Needed to Improve the Use of Private Security Providers', available at: http://www.gao.gov/new.items/d06865t.pdf, last accessed March 27, 2008.

–, July 2008. 'Rebuilding Iraq: DOD and State Department Have Improved Oversight and Coordination of Private Security Contractors in Iraq, but Further Actions are Needed to Sustain Improvements', available at: http://www.gao.gov/new.items/d08966.pdf, last accessed August 29, 2008.

Greig, Michael J., 2001. 'Moments of Opportunity', *Journal of Conflict Resolution* 45(6), pp. 691–718.

–, 2005. 'Stepping Into the Frey: When do Mediators Mediate?', *Journal of Conflict Resolution* 49(2), pp. 249–266.

Greig, Michael J. & Paul F. Diehl, 2006. 'Softening Up: Making Conflicts More Amenable to Diplomacy', *International Interactions* 32(4), pp. 355–384.

Greig, Michael J. & Patrick M. Regan, 2008. 'When do They Say Yes? An Analysis of the Willingness to Offer and Accept Mediation in Civil Wars', *International Studies Quarterly* 52(4), pp. 759–781.

Gunasekera, S.L. & G. Dayasiri, 2006. 'Bauer a Facilitator or Agent for Int'l Terrorism?', *The Island*, Colombo, September 9

Gunner, Göran & Erik Lindberg *et al.* (eds.), 1985. *Längtan till Ararat. En bok om Armenien och armenisk identitet.* Göteborg: Gothia.

Gunning, Jeroen, 2008. *Hamas in Politics: Democracy, Religion and Violence.* New York: Columbia University Press.

Hampson, Fen Osler, 1996. *Nurturing Peace. Why Peace Settlements Succeed or Fail.* Washington, DC.: United States Institute of Peace Press.

Hampson, Fen Osler, 2002. 'Preventive Diplomacy at the United Nations and Beyond', in Fen Osler Hampson & David Malone (eds.), *From Reaction to Conflict Prevention: Opportunities for the UN System.* Boulder, CO: Lynne Rienner, pp. 139–158.

Hampson, Fen Osler & David Malone (eds.), 2002. *From Reaction to Conflict Prevention: Opportunities for the UN System.* Boulder, CO: Lynne Rienner.

Hanley, Lynne, 1991. *Writing War: Fiction, Gender and Memory.* Amherst: University of Massachusetts Press.

Harbom, Lotta (ed.), 2007. *States in Armed Conflict 2006.* Uppsala: Department of Peace and Conflict Research, Uppsala University.

Hardin, Russell, 2002. 'Whither Political Science?', *Political Science & Politics* 35(2), pp. 183–186.

Harkavy, Robert E. and Stephanie G. Neuman, 2001. *Warfare and the Third World.* New York, N.Y.: Palgrave.

Heaton, J. Ricou, 2005. 'Civilians at War: Reexamining the Status of Civilians Accompanying the Armed Forces', *Air Force Law Review* 57, pp.157–208.

Heldt, Birger, 1999. 'Domestic Politics, Absolute Deprivation, and the Use of Armed Force in Interstate Territorial Disputes, 1950–1990', *Journal of Conflict Resolution* 43(4), pp. 451–478.

–, 2008a. 'Trends from 1948–2005: How to View the Relation between the United Nations and Non-UN Entities', in Don Daniel (ed.), *Prospects for Peace Operations: Institutional and National Dimensions.* Washington DC.: Georgetown University Press, pp. 9–26.

–, 2008b. 'Preventive Diplomacy in Emerging Intrastate Conflicts: Some Historical Patterns', in Anders Mellbourn (ed.), *Third Parties and Conflict Prevention.* Stockholm and Brussels: Madariaga Foundation, pp. 205–222.

Helgesen, Vidar, 2007. 'How Peace Diplomacy Lost Post 9/11: What Implications are there for Norway?' *Oslo Files on Security and Defence,* no. 3.

Hellesund, Tone & Inger Marie Okkenhaug (eds.), 2003. *Erobring og overskridelse. De nye kvinnene inntar verden 1870–1940.* Oslo: Unipub Forlag.

Herman, Judith, 1992. *Trauma and Recovery.* New York: Basic Books.

Hibou, Béatrice (ed.), 2004. *Privatizing the State.* New York: Columbia University Press.

Hills, Alice, 2002. 'Hearts and Minds Or Search and Destroy? Controlling Civilians in Urban Operations', *Small Wars and Insurgencies* 13(1), pp. 1–24.

Höglund, Anna T., Karin Haglund & Martin Smedjeback (eds.), 2004. *Ickevåld och genus.* Stockholm: Kristna Fredsrörelsen.

Höglund, Anna T., 2004. 'Teologi, genus och rättfärdiga krig', in Karin Aggestam (ed.), *(O)rättfärdiga Krig.* Lund: Studentlitteratur.

Höglund, Kristine, 2004. *Violence in the Midst of Peace Negotiations: Cases from Guatemala, Northern Ireland, South Africa and Sri Lanka.* Uppsala: Department of Peace and Conflict Research, Uppsala University.

Höglund, Kristine, 2008. 'Violence in War-to-Democracy Transitions', in Anna Jarstad & Timothy D. Sisk (eds.), *War-to-Democracy Transitions: Dilemmas of Peacebuilding.* Cambridge: Cambridge University Press.

Höglund, Kristine & Isak Svensson, 2008a. 'Damned if You Do, and Damned if You Don't: Nordic Involvement and Third-Party Neutrality in Sri Lanka', *International Negotiation* 13(2), pp. 341–364.

–, 2008b. Interests of the Intermediary: Norwegian Mediation in Sri Lanka 2000–2006, unpublished paper.

Hollis, Rosemary, 2004. 'The Israeli-Palestinian Road Block: Can Europeans Make a Difference?', *International Affairs,* 2 pp. 191–201.

Holmqvist, Caroline, 2005. 'Private Security Companies: The Case for Regulation', *SIPRI Policy Paper No. 9,* January 2005.

Holmes, John, DSO, OBE, MC, Maj. Gen. (Retd). Director of International Affairs, Erinys International. Interviewed in London, May 15, 2007.

Holsti, Kalevi, 1996. *State, War and the State of War.* Cambridge: Cambridge University Press.

Holzgrefe, J.L. & Robert O. Keohane (eds.), 2003. *Humanitarian Intervention: Ethical, Legal, and Political Dilemmas.* Cambridge: Cambridge University Press.

House Committee on Oversight and Government Reform, February 2007: 'Additional Information for Hearing on Private Security Contractors', available at: http://oversight.house.gov/documents/20070207112331–22533.pdf, last accessed October 15, 2007

–, October 2007: 'Additional Information about Blackwater USA', available at: http://oversight.house.gov/documents/20071001121609.pdf, last accessed October 15, 2007.

House of Commons, 2001. 'Operation Enduring Freedom and the Conflict in Afghanistan: An Update', *Research Paper 01/81*, 31 October, available at: http://www.parliment.uk/commons/lib/research/rp2001/rp01-81.pdf, last accessed 16 December 2008.

Hovannisian, Richard (ed.), 1992. *The Armenian Genocide: History, Politics, Ethics.* Houndmills and London: Macmillan.

Hroub, Khaled, 2006. 'A "New Hamas" Through its New Documents', *Journal of Palestine Studies* XXXV,(4).

Hultvall, John, 1991. *Mission och vision i Orienten. Svenska Missionsförbundets mission i Transkaukasien – Persien 1882–1921.* Stockholm: Verbum.

Human Rights Watch, 2004. *LTTE Commitments to End the Recruitment and Use of Child Soldiers,* November issue.

Human Rights First, 2008. *Private Security Contractors at War: Ending the Culture of Impunity.* available at: http://www.humanrightsfirst.org.

Human Security Report, 2005. War and Peace in the 21st Century, available at: http://www.humansecurityreport.info/index.php?option=content&task=view&id=28&Itemid=63, last accessed: 3 March 2009.

Huntington, Samuel P., 1957. *The Soldier and the State: The Theory and Politics of Civil-Military Relations,* 6th printing (1979), Cambridge, Mass. and London: Harvard University Press.

Huth, Paul K., 1996. *Standing Your Ground: Territorial Disputes and International Conflict.* Ann Arbor M.I.: University of Michigan Press.

Hynes, Samuel, 1990. *A War Imagined: The First World War and English Culture.* London: The Bodely Head.

Iklé, Fred Charles, 1964. *How Nations Negotiate.* New York: Praeger.

Independent, 2005. 'Lynndie England in Plea Bargain to Cut Prison Term', *The Independent,* 2 May, available at: http://www.aftenposten.no/english/local/article736190.ece?service=print, last accessed 16 December 2008.

International Crisis Group, 2008. 'Sri Lanka's Return to War: Limiting the Damage', *Asia Report,* no. 146.

International Security Assistance Force, *International Security Assistance Force (ISAF),* available at: http://www.nato.int/issues/isaf/index.html, last accessed 16 December 2008.

International Security Assistance Force, *Reconstruction and Development (R&D),* available at: http://www.nato.int/isaf/topics/recon–dev/index.html, last accessed 16 December 2008.

IPOA. (2007) *State of the Peace and Stability Operations Industry Survey 2006.* available at: http://www.ipoaonline.org

Isenberg, David, 2004. 'A Fistful of Contractors: The Case for a Pragmatic Assessment of Private Military Companies in Iraq', *BASIC Research Report 2004/4*, available at: http://www.basicint.org/pubs/Research/2004PMC.htm.

–, 2007. 'A government in Search of Cover: Private Military Companies in Iraq', in Simon Chesterman & Chia Lehnardt (eds.) *From Mercenaries to Market: The Rise and Regulation of Private Military Companies.* Oxford: Oxford University Press, pp. 82–94.

Jackman, Simon, 1999. In and Out Of War: The Statistical Analysis of Discrete Serial Data on International Conflict. Stanford CA.: Department of Political Science, Stanford University, Unpublished manuscript.

Jagland, Thorbjorn, 2008. 'Våre egne myter (Our Own Myths)' *Aftenposten*, January 4.

Jakobsen, Peter V., 2005. *PRTs in Afghanistan: Successful but Not Sufficient.* Copenhagen: Danish Institute for International Studies.

Jarstad, Anna & Timothy D. Sisk (ed.), 2008. *From War to Democracy: Dilemmas of Peacebuilding.* Cambridge: Cambridge University Press.

Johansson, Alma, 1924. *Bilder från K.M.A.:s missionsfält. K.M.A. 1894–1924.* Stockholm: Kvinnliga Missionsarbetare.

–, 1930. *Ett folk i landsflykt. Ett år ur armeniernas historia.* Stockholm: Kvinnliga Missionsarbetare.

–, 1934. 'Tidevarv komma, tidevarv försvinna', *K.M.A. Minnesskrift 1894–1934.* Stockholm: Kvinnliga Missionsarbetare.

–, 1944. *Budkavle kommer, budkavle går. Jubileumsskrift 1894–1944.* Stockholm: Kvinnliga Missionsarbetare.

Joint Publication 3–07.3, Peace Operations.

Joint Publication 3–24, Counterinsurgency 2008, draft.

Kaldor, Mary, 1999. *New and Old Wars. Organized Violence in a Global Era.* London: Polity Press.

–, 2003. *Global Civil Society. An Answer to War.* Cambridge: Polity Press.

Keenan, Alan, 2007. 'The Trouble with Evenhandedness: On the Politics of Human Rights and Peace Advocacy in Sri Lanka', in M. Feher (ed.) *Nongovernmental Politics.* Brooklyn, New York: Zone Books, pp. 88–117.

Keethaponcalan, S.I., 2005. 'The Ethnic Conflict in Sri Lanka and the Dynamics of Third Party Activity', in J. Uyangoda (ed.), *Conflict, Conflict Resolution & Peace Building.* Colombo: Colombo University.

Kelleher, Ann & James Larry Taulbee, 2006. 'Bridging the Gap: Building Peace Norwegian Style', *Peace & Change* 31(4), pp. 479–505.

Kemp, Geoffrey, 2003. 'Europe's Middle East Challenges', *The Washington Quarterly* 27(1), pp. 163–177.

Kennedy, Paul & Jay Winter (eds.), 2004. *America and the Armenian Genocide of 1915.* Cambridge: Cambridge University Press.

King, Charles, 1997. 'Ending Civil Wars', *Adelphi Paper 308.* Oxford: Oxford University Press.

Kinsey, C., 2005. 'Challenging International Law: a Dilemma of Private Security Companies', *Conflict, Security & Development* 5(3), pp. 269–293.

—, 2006. *Corporate Soldiers and International Security: The Rise of Private Military Companies*. Abingdon: Routledge.

Kleibor, Marieke, 1996. 'Understanding Success and Failure of International Mediation', *Journal of Conflict Resolution* 40(2), pp. 360–389.

Kocs, Stephen A., 1995. 'Territorial Disputes and Interstate War, 1945–1987', *Journal of Politics* 57(1), pp. 159–175.

Kohn, Richard H., 1997: 'How Democracies Control the Military', *Journal of Democracy* 8(4), pp. 140–153.

Kostic, Roland, 2008. *Ambivalent Peace. External Peacebuilding, Threatened Identity and Reconciliation in Bosnia-Herzegovina*. Uppsala: Department of Peace and Conflict Research, Uppsala University.

Kreutz, Joakim, 2005. *Armed Conflict Termination Dataset Codebook. Version 1.0* Uppsala: Department of Peace and Conflict Research, Uppsala University.

Kriesberg, Louis, 1996. 'Coordinating Intermediary Peace Efforts', *Negotiation Journal* 12(4), pp. 341–352.

Kydd, Andrew & Barbara F. Walter, 2002. 'Sabotaging the Peace: The Politics of Extremist Violence', *International Organization* 56(2), pp. 263–296.

Leander, Anna, 2005. 'The Market for Force and Public Security: The Destabilizing Consequences of Private Military Companies', *Journal of Peace Research* 42(5), pp. 605–622.

—, 2006. *Eroding State Authority? Private Military Companies and the Legitimate Use of Force*. Rome: Centro Militare di Studi Strategici, available at: http://www.isn.ethz.ch/pubs/ph/details.cfm?lng=en&id=20511.

—, 2007a. 'The Impunity of Private Authority: Understanding the Circumscribed Efforts to Introduce PMC Accountability' *ISA* Chicago 28 February-3 March, available at: http://www.cbs.dk/content/view/pub/38570.

—, 2007b. 'Regulating the Role of PMCs in Shaping Security and Politics', in Simon Chesterman & Chia Lehnardt (eds.) *From Mercenaries to Markets: The Rise and Regulation of Private Military Companies*. Oxford: Oxford University Press, pp. 49–64.

—, 2008. *Portraits in Practice: The Politics of Outsourcing Security*. Under review, forthcoming, available at: http://www.cbs.dk/content/view/pub/38570.

Larsdotter, Kersti, 2007. 'Culture and the Outcome of Military Intervention: Developing some Hypotheses', in Jan Angstrom & Isabelle Duyvesteyn (eds.), *Understanding Victory and Defeat in Contemporary War*. London: Routledge, pp. 206–223.

—, 2008. 'Exploring the Utility of Armed Force in Peace Operations: German and British Approaches in Northern Afghanistan', *Small Wars & Insurgencies* 19(3), pp. 352–373.

Lederach, John Paul, 1995. *Preparing for Peace. Conflict Transformation Across Cultures.* New York: Syracuse University Press.

–, 1997. *Building Peace: Sustainable Reconciliation in Divided Societies.* Washington, D.C.: United States Institute of Peace.

Lieberfeld, Daniel, 1995. 'Small Is Credible: Norway's Niche in International Dispute Settlement', *Negotiation Journal* 11(3), pp. 201–207.

Lindberg, Erik 1985. 'Svensk Armenienpolitik', in Göran Gunner & Erik Lindberg *et al.* (eds.) *Längtan till Ararat. En bok om Armenien och armenisk identitet.* Göteborg: Gothia, pp. 264–276.

Lopez, Andrea M., 2007. 'Engaging Or Withdrawing, Winning Or Losing? The Contradictions of Counterinsurgency Policy in Afghanistan and Iraq', *Third World Quarterly* 28(2), pp. 245–260.

Lorentzen, Lois Ann & Jennifer Turpin (eds.), 1998. *The Women and War Reader.* New York and London: New York University Press.

Lund, Michael, 1996. *Preventing Violent Conflict.* Washington DC.: United States Institute for Peace

–, 2008. 'Conflict Prevention: Theory in Pursuit of Policy and Practice,' in Jacob Bercovitch, Victor Kremenyk & I. William Zartman (eds.), *Handbook of Conflict Resolution.* Thousand Oaks, CA.: Sage Publications, pp. 285–321.

Lundqvist, Lennart J., 1988. 'Privatization: Towards a Concept of Comparative Policy Analysis', *Journal of Public Policy* 8(1), pp. 1–19.

Lunstead, Jeffrey, 2007. *The United States' Role in Sri Lanka's Peace Process, 2002–2006.* Colombo: Asia Foundation.

MacFarquhar, Emily, Robert I. Rotberg & Martha A. Chen, 1995. 'Introduction', in Robert I. Rotberg (eds.), *Vigilance and Vengeance. NGOs Preventing Ethnic Conflict in Divided Societies,* Washington, D.C: Brookings Institution Press.

MacGinty, Roger, 2006. *No War, No Peace. The Rejuvenation of Stalled Peace Processes and Peace Accords.* Houndsmills & New York: Palgrave MacMillan.

Malkasian, Carter, 2008. 'Did the United States Need More Forces in Iraq? Evidence from Al Anbar', *Defence Studies* 8(1), pp. 78–104.

Maloney, Sean M., 2005. 'Afghanistan Four Years on: An Assessment', *Parameters* 35(3).

Mandel, Robert, 2002. *Armies without States: The Privatization of Security.* Boulder CO.: Lynne Reinner.

Mansfield, Edward D. & Jack Snyder, 2007. 'The Sequencing 'Fallacy'', *Journal of Democracy* 18(1), pp. 5–9.

Markusen, Ann R., 2003. 'The Case Against Privatizing National Security', *Governance: An International Journal of Policy, Administration, and Institutions* 16, pp. 471–501.

Martin, Harriet, 2006. *Kings of Peace, Pawns of War: The Untold Story of Peace-Making.* New York & London: Continuum.

Maundi, Mohammed O., I. William Zartman, Gilbert Khadiagala & Kwaku Nuamah, 2006. *Getting In: Mediator's Entry into the Settlement of African Conflicts*. Washington D.C.: USIP Press.

McGilvray, Dennis B. & Mirak Raheem, 2007. 'Muslim Perspectives on the Sri Lankan Conflict', *Policy Studies*. Washington: East-West Center.

Meintjes, Sheila, Anu Pillay & Meredeth Turshen (eds.), 2002. *The Aftermath. Women in Post-Conflict Transformation*. London & New York: Zed Books.

Mellbourn, Anders (ed.), 2008. *Third Parties and Conflict Prevention*. Stockholm and Brussels: Madariaga Foundation.

Melman, Billie, 1992. *Women's Orients: English Women and the Middle East, 1718–1918*. London: Macmillan.

Miall, Hugh, Oliver Ramsbotham & Tom Woodhouse, 1999. *Contemporary Conflict Resolution*. Cambridge: Polity Press & Oxford: Blackwell Publishers Ltd.

Miller, Rory, 2006. 'Troubled Neighbours: The EU and Israel', *Israel Affairs* 12(4), pp. 642–664.

Milliard, Major Todd S., 2003. 'Overcoming Post-Colonial Myopia: A Call to Recognize and Regulate Private Military Companies', *Military Law Review* 1.

Ministry of Rural Rehabilitation and Development, *Balkh, Provincial Profile*, available at: http://www.mrrd.gov.af/nabdp/Provincial%20Profiles/Balkh%20PDP%20Provincial%20profile.pdf, last accessed 16 December 2008.

Minow, Martha, 2003. 'Public and Private Partnerships: Accounting for the New Religion', *Harvard Law Review* 116, pp. 1229–1270.

Mitchell, Christopher R., 1988. 'The Motives for Mediation', in C.R. Mitchell and K. Webb (eds.), *New Approaches to International Mediation*. London: Greenwood Press.

–, 1993. 'External Peace-Making Initiatives and Intra-National Conflict', in M.I. Midlarsky (ed.) *The Internationalization of Communal Strife*. London & New York: Routledge, pp. 275–296.

–, 1995. 'The Right Moment: Notes on Four Models of "Ripeness"', *Paradigms. The Kent Journal of International Relations* 9(2), pp. 35–52.

Mohamed, Rabie, 1992. 'The US–PLO Dialogue: The Swedish Connection', *Journal of Palestine Studies* 21(4), pp. 54–66.

Møller, Bjørn, 2005. 'Privatisation of Conflict, Security and War', *DIIS Working Paper*, No. 2005/2.

Montreaux document, 2008, available at: http://www.icrc.org/web/eng/siteengo.nsf/htmlall/montreux-document-170908/$FILE/Montreux-Document.pdf.

Moranian, Suzanne Elizabeth, 1992. 'Bearing Witness: The Missionary Archives as Evidence of the Armenian Genocide', in Richard Hovannisian, (ed.), *The Armenian Genocide: History, Politics, Ethics.* Houndmills & London: Macmillan, pp 103–128.

Morgenthau, Henry, 1918. *Ambassador Morgenthau's Story.* New York: Doubleday.

Mosse, George L., 1990. *Fallen Soldiers. Reshaping the Memories of the World Wars.* New York: Oxford University Press.

Mueller, John, 2000. 'The Banality of "Ethnic War"', *International Security* 25(1), pp. 42–70.

Musah, Adel-Fatau, 2002. 'Privatization of Security: Arms Proliferation and the Process of State Collapse in Africa', *Development and Change* 33(5), pp. 911–933.

Musah, Abdel-Fatau & Kayode J. Fayemi (eds.), 2000. *Mercenaries: An African Security Dilemma.* London: Pluto Press.

Münkler, Herfried, 2005. *The New Wars.* Trans. by Patrick Camiller. Cambridge & Malden: Polity Press.

Nassibian, Akaby, 1984. *Britain and the Armenian Question 1915–1923.* Croom Helm. London and New York: St. Martin's Press.

NATO AJP–3.4.1, Peace Support Operations, 2001.

Natsios, Andrew, 1995. 'NGOs and the UN System in Complex Humanitarian Emergencies: Conflict or Cooperation', *Third World Quarterly*, 16 (3), pp. 405–421.

New York Times, 2007. 'F.B.I. Says Guards Killed 14 Iraqis Without Cause', November 13, available at: www.nytimes.com/2007/11/14/world/middleeast/14blackwater.html?–r=1&oref=slogin, last accessed September 24, 2008.

–, 2008. '5 Guards Face U.S. Charges in Iraq Deaths', December 6, available at: http://www.nytimes.com/2008/12/06/washington/06blackwater.html?partner=rss&emc=rss, last accessed December 8, 2008.

Nicolaidis, Kalypso, 1995. 'International Preventive Action: Developing a Strategic Framework', in Robert I. Rotberg (ed.), *Vigilance and Vengeance. NGOs Preventing Ethnic Conflict in Divided Societies.* Washington DC.: Brookings Institution Press.

Nikitin, Alexander, 2008. 'Principles for elaborating new United Nations legal instruments (including Convention) on regulation of PMSCs (private military and security companies)'. *The privatisation of security*, Copenhagen 24–25 November.

North Atlantic Treaty Organization, 'ISAF Contributing Nations', available at: http://www.nato.int/ISAF/structure/nations/index.html, last accessed 16 December 2008.

North Atlantic Treaty Organization, *Expansion of NATO's Presence in Afghanistan*, available at: http://www.nato.int/isaf/topics/expansion/index.html, last accessed 3 March 2008.

North, Douglass C., 1990. *Institutions, Institutional Change and Economic Performance*. Cambridge: Cambridge University Press.

Norwegian Government, Ministry of Trade and Industry, 2008. Oppstart av forhandlinger mellom EFTA og India (Negotiation between EFTA and India Begins), Press Release No. 05/08, January 21, Oslo.

Ohlson, Thomas, 1998. *Power Politics and Peace Policies: Intra-State Conflict Resolution in Southern Africa*. Uppsala: Department of Peace and Conflict Research, Uppsala University.

Oklahoma Daily, The, 2007. Interview with Colin Powell by Will Prescott, September 11, available at: http://hub.ou.edu/multimedia/index. html?bcpid=1155389226, last accessed 7 Oct. 2008.

Okkenhaug, Inger Marie (ed.), 2003. *Gender, Race and Religion. Nordic Missions 1860–1940*. Uppsala: University of Uppsala.

–, 2007. 'Midtøstens religion og kultur i europeiske framstillinger', in Per Steinar Raaen & Olav Skevik (eds.) *Fiendebilder – historie og samtid*. Stiklestad: Stiklestad nasjonale kultursenter.

Olonisakin, Fumni, 2000. 'Arresting the Tide of Mercenaries: Prospects for Regional Control', in Abdel-Fatau Musah & Kayode J. Fayemi (eds.) *Mercenaries: An African Security Dilemma*. London: Pluto Press, pp. 233–257.

Olson, Lara, 2006. 'Fighting for Humanitarian Space: NGOs in Afghanistan', *Journal of Military and Strategic Studies*, 9(1), available at: http://www.jmss.org/2006/2006fall/articles/olson–ngo-afghanistan.pdf, last accessed 15 December 2008.

Orjuela, Camilla, 2008. *Identity Politics of Peacebuilding: Civil Society in Sri Lanka's Violent Conflict*. Los Angeles, London, New York, Singapore: Sage.

Österberg, Eva & Marie Lindstedt Cronberg (eds.), 2005. *Kvinnor och våld. En mångtydig kulturhistoria*. Lund: Nordic Academic Press.

Palestinian Center for Policy and Survey Research, available at: http://www.pcpsr.org/survey/polls/2007

Palihapitiya, Madhawa, 2007. 'Of a Norwegian Summer and a Viking Intervention in Sri Lanka', *Asian Journal of Public Affairs* 1(1), pp. 39–53.

Parfitt, George, 1988. *Fiction of the First World War*. London: Faber & Faber.

Paris, Roland, 2004. *At War's End. Building Peace After Civil Conflict*. Cambridge: Cambridge University Press.

Pelton, Robert Young, 2006. *Licensed to Kill: Hired Guns in the War on Terror*. New York: Crown Publishers.

Percy, Sarah, 2006. 'Regulating the Private Security Industry', *Adelphi Paper 384*, International Institute for Strategic Studies. Abingdon: Routledge.

Perera, Jehan, 2004. *Japan Has a Bigger Role to Play in the Peace Process Current Situation*, July 24, available at: http.www.peace-srilanka.org).

Perito, Robert M., 2005. *The U.S. Experience with Provincial Reconstruction Teams in Afghanistan*. Washington DC.: United States Institute of Peace.

Philipson, Liz, 2001. 'Negotiating Processes in Sri Lanka', *Marga Monograph Series on Ethnic Reconciliation*, No 2. Colombo: Marga Institute.

–, 2005. 'Engaging Armed Groups: The Challenge of Asymmetries', in R. Ricigliano (ed.) *Choosing to Engage: Armed Groups and Peace Processes*. London: Conciliation Resources.

Pillar, Paul R., 1983. *Negotiating Peace: War Termination as a Bargaining Process*. Princeton: Princeton University.

Pouligny, Béatrice, 2006. *Peace Operations Seen from Below: UN Missions and Local People*. London: Hurst & Company.

Power, Samantha, 2002. *'A Problem from Hell'. America and the Age of Genocide*. New York: Basic Books.

Pruitt, Dean G. & Sung Hee Kim, (eds.), 2004. *Social Conflict: Escalation, Stalemate, and Settlement*. New York: McGraw Hill.

Quinn, David, Jonathan Wilkenfeld, Kathleen Smarick & Victor Asal, 2006. 'Power Play: Mediation in Symmetric and Asymmetric International Crises', *International Interactions* 32(4), pp. 441–470.

Raitt, Suzanne & Trudi Tate (eds.), 1997. *Writing Women: Identity and Ideology in the First World War*. London: Routledge.

Rasor, Dina & Robert Bauman, 2007. *Betraying Our Troops: The Destructive Results of Privatizing War*. New York: Palgrave.

Regan, Patrick & Alan Stam, 2000. 'In the Nick of Time: Conflict Management, Mediation Timing, and the Duration of Interstate Disputes', *International Studies Quarterly* 44(2), pp. 239–260.

Regan, Patrick & Aysegul Aydin, 2006. 'Diplomacy and Other Forms of Intervention in Civil Wars', *Journal of Conflict Resolution* 50(5), pp. 736–756.

Reno, William, 2004. 'The Privatisation of Sovereignty and the Survival of Weak States', in Béatrice Hibou (ed.) *Privatizing the State*. New York: Columbia University Press, pp. 95–119.

Reychler, Luc & Thania Paffenholz (eds.), 2001. *Peace Building. A Field Guide*. Boulder: Lynne Rienner Publishers.

Richmond, Oliver, 1998. 'Devious Objectives and the Disputants' View of International Mediation', *Journal of Peace Research* 35(6), pp. 707–722.

–, 2006. 'The Linkage between Devious Objectives and Spoiling Behaviour in Peace Processes', in Edwards Newman & Oliver Richmond (eds.), *Spoilers and Peace Processes: Conflict Settlement and Devious Objectives*. Tokyo: UN University Press.

Ricigliano, R. (ed.), 2005. *Choosing to Engage: Armed Groups and Peace Processes*. London: Conciliation Resources.

Roe, Paul, 2000. 'The Intrastate Security Dilemma: Ethnic Conflict as a "Tragedy"?', *Journal of Peace Research* 36(2), pp. 183–202.

Ross, Marc Howard, 1997. 'Culture and Identity in Comparative Political Analysis', in Mark Irving Lichbach & Alan S. Zuckerman (eds.) *Compara-*

tive Politics. Rationality, Culture, and Structure. Cambridge: Cambridge University Press.

Rovik, Falk, 2005. 'Norway: A Terrorist Safe Haven?', in *Peace in Sri Lanka: Obstacles and Opportunities*, Nugegoda: World Alliance for Peace in Sri Lanka.

Ruddick, Sara, 1989. *Maternal Thinking: Toward a Politics of Peace*. Boston: Beacon Press.

Ruggie, John Gerard, 1998. *Constructing the World Polity: Essays on International Institutionalization*. Abingdon & New York: Routledge.

Rupesinghe, Kumar, 2006. 'Interview with Erik Solheim, Minister of International Development', in K. Rupesinghe (ed.), *Negotiating Peace in Sri Lanka: Efforts, Failures and Lessons. Volume Two*. Colombo: Foundation of Co-Existence, pp. 339–354.

Said, Edward W., 1978. *Orientalism*. London: Routledge & Kegan Paul.

–, 1993. *Culture and Imperialism*. London: Chatto & Windus.

Salem, Richard, 1982. 'Community Dispute Resolution Through Outside Intervention', *Peace & Change* 8(2/3).

Saravanantha, Muttukrishna, 2007a. 'Norwegian and British Interventions in the Sri Lankan Conflict: A Sorry Tale of Misinformation and Misunderstanding', *Groundviews*, December 17.

–, 2007b. 'In Pursuit of the Mythical Sate of Tamil Eelam: A Rejoinder to Kristian Stokke', *Third World Quarterly* 28(6), pp. 1185–1195.

Saravanthan, Muttukrishna & Indra de Soysa, 2007. 'Nyttige idioter fra nord' (Useful Imbeciles from the North), *Aftenposten*, December 30

Scahill, Jeremy, 2007. 'Iraqis Sue Blackwater for Baghdad Killings', *The Nation*, October 11, 2007, available at: http://www.thenation.com/doc/20071029/scahill, last accessed 24 September, 2008.

Schetter, Conrad, Rainer Glassner & Masood Karokhail, 2007. 'Beyond Warlordism: The Local Security Architecture in Afghanistan', *Internationale Politik und Gesellschaft*, 2, pp. 136–152, available at: http://www.fes.de/IPG/inhalt–d/pdf/10–Schetter–US.pdf>, last accessed 16 December 2008.

Schulz, Helena Lindholm, 1999. 'Identity Conflicts and Their Resolution: The Oslo Agreement and Palestinian Identities' in H. Wiberg & C.P. Scherrer, *Ethnicity and Intra-State Conflict. Types, Causes and Peace Strategies*. Aldershot: Ashgate.

Schulz, Michael, 1996. *Israel Between Conflict and Accommodation. A Study of a Multi-Melting Pot Process*. Göteborg: Padrigu Thesis Series (dissertation thesis).

–, 2007. 'Hamas Between Sharia Rule and Democracy', in Ashok Swain, Ramses Amer & Joakim Öjendal (eds.). *Globalization and Challenges to Peacebuilding*. London: Antheme Press.

–, 2008, 'Reconciliation through education—Experiences from the Israeli-Palestinian Conflict', *Journal of Peace Education* 5(1), pp. 33–48.

Scoville, Ryan M., 2006. 'Toward an Accountability-based Definition of "Mercenary"', *Georgetown Journal of International Law* 37, pp. 541–582.

Shlaim, Avi, 2005. 'Europe and the Israeli-Palestinian Conflict', *Occasional Paper*. Oxford: Oxford Research Group.

Singer, P. W., 2003. *Corporate Warriors. The Rise of the Privatized Military Industry.* Ithaca & London: Cornell University Press.

–, 2004. 'The Private Military Industry in Iraq: What We Have Learned and Where to Go Next?', *Geneva Centre for the Democratic Control of Armed Forces (DCAF)*, November 2004, Geneva, available at: http://www.dcaf.ch/–docs/pp04–private-military.pdf, last accessed January 31, 2007.

–, 2007a. 'Can't Win With 'Em, Can't Go To War Without 'Em: Private Military Contractors and Counterinsurgency', *Foreign Policy at Brookings, Policy paper* No. 4.

–, 2007b. 'The Law Catches Up to Private Militaries (and embeds too)', *DefenseTech*, available at: http://www.defensetech.org/archives/003123.html.

Småberg, Maria, 2005. *Ambivalent Friendship. Anglican Conflict Handling and Education for Peace in Jerusalem 1920–1948.* Lund: Lund University.

Smith, Karen E., 2007. 'Promoting Peace in the Backyard?', *The International Spectator* 42(4), pp. 594–596.

Special Inspector General for Iraq Reconstruction (SIGIR), 2004. available at: sigir.mil/reports/quarterlyreports/ Jul04/table–j–1–verified– contracts– updated.pdf, July 2004, last accessed 10 February, 2007.

–, 2007. *Report*, January 2007, available at: http://www.sigir.mil/reports/quarterlyreports/Jan07/Default.aspx, last accessed, 15 October, 2007.

Spicer, Tim, 2006. 'The Private Company in Modern Conflict', speech delivered at *the RUSI conference on ROE*, London, July 18.

Spiegel, Der Online, 2006. 'Skull Images Shock Germany', *Spiegel Online*, 26 October 2006, available at: http://www.spiegel.de/international/0,1518,444879,00.html, last accessed 16 December 2008.

–, 2006. 'Macabre Photos Disgrace German Military', *Spiegel Online,* 25 October, 2006, available at: http://www.spiegel.de/international/0,1518,444610,00.html, last accessed 16 December 2008.

Spiegel, Peter, 2007. 'Gates: Security Contractors Conflict with U.S. Mission in Iraq', *Los Angeles Times*, October 19.

Stanley, Brian, 1990. *The Bible and the Flag. Protestant Missions & British Imperialism in the Nineteenth & Twentieth Centuries.* London: Apollos.

Statistics Office Afghanistan, 2006. 'Settled Population by Civil Division (Urban and Rural) and Sex 2005–2006, available at: http://www.csoaf.net/cso/documents/estimated%20population%201384.xls>, last accessed 1 April 2008.

Stedman, Stephen J., 1995. 'Alchemy for a New World Order. Overselling Preventive Diplomacy', *Foreign Affairs* 74(3) pp. 14–20.

–, 1996. 'Negotiation and Mediation in Internal Conflict', in Michael E. Brown (ed.), *The International Dimensions of Internal Conflict*. Cambridge: The MIT Press.

–, 1997. 'Spoiler Problems in Peace Processes', *International Security* 22(2), pp. 5–53.

Stedman, S. J., D. Rothchild & E. M. Cousens, 2002. *Ending Civil Wars. The Implementation of Peace Agreements*. Boulder, London: Lynne Rienner Publishers.

Stern, Paul C. & Daniel Druckman, 2000. 'Evaluating Interventions in History', *International Studies Review* 2(1), pp. 33–63.

Stern, Paul C. & Daniel Druckman (eds.), 2000. *International Conflict Resolution After the Cold War*. Washington, D.C.: National Academy Press.

Stokke, Kristian, 2007. 'War by Other Means', *Third World Quarterly* 28(6), pp. 1197–1201.

–, 2008. Bistandsdebatt på lavt nivå (Aid Debate on a Low Level). *Aftenposten*, December 8.

Sturfelt, Lina, 2005. 'Den andras lidande. Kvinnor som våldsoffer och förövare i första världskriget', in Eva Österberg & Marie Lindstedt Cronberg (eds.), *Kvinnor och våld. En mångtydig kulturhistoria*. Lund: Nordic Academic Press, pp. 219–241.

–, 2008. *Eldens Återsken. Första Världskriget i svensk föreställningsvärld*. Lund: Sekel Bokförlag.

Svensson, Isak, 2007. *Elusive Peacemakers*. Uppsala: Department of Peace and Conflict Research, Uppsala University.

Swain, Ashok, Ramses Amer & Joakim Öjendal (eds.), 2007. *Globalization and Challenges to Peacebuilding*. London: Antheme Press.

Swedish Armed Forces, 2008. 'Afghanistan', available at: http://www2.mil.se/sv/Insatser/Afghanistan/, last accessed 31 March 2008.

Talentino, Andrea Kathryn, 2007. 'Perceptions of Peacebuilding: The Dynamics of Imposer and Imposed Upon', *International Studies Perspectives* 8(2), pp. 152–171.

Tambiah, Stanley Jeyeraja, 1992. *Buddhism Betrayed? Religion, Politics, and Violence in Sri Lanka*. Chicago: The University of Chicago Press.

Tamimi, Azzam, 2007. *Hamas Unwritten Chapters*. London: Hurst & Co. Ltd.

Tate, Trudi, 1998. *Modernism, History and the First World War*. Manchester: Manchester University Press.

Tavares, Rodrigo & Michael Schulz, 2006. 'The Intervention of Regional Organizations in Peace Building', in Philippe De Lombaerde (ed.), *Indicators of Regional Integration*. London: Routledge.

Thomson, Janice E. 1995. 'State Sovereignty in International Relations', *International Studies Quarterly* 39, pp. 213–233.

Thornton, Rod, 2000. 'The Role of Peace Support Operations Doctrine in the British Army', *International Peacekeeping* 7(2), pp. 41–62.

–, 2004. 'The British Army and the Origins of its Minimum Force Philosophy', *Small Wars & Insurgencies* 15(1), pp. 83–106.

Time Magazine, 2008. 'Verbatim' 171(21), 26 May.

Tocci, Nathalie, 2005. 'Conflict Resolution in the Neighbourhood: Comparing EU Involvement in Turkey's Kurdish Question and in the Israeli-Palestinian Conflict', *Mediterranean Politics*, 10(2), pp. 25–46.

–, 2007. *The EU and Conflict Resolution: Promoting Peace in the Backyard.* London and New York: Routledge.

Touval, Saadia, 2003. 'Mediation and Foreign Policy', *International Studies Review* 5(4), pp. 91–95.

Touval, Saadia & I. William Zartman, 2001. 'International Mediation in the Post-Cold War Era', in C. A. Crocker, F. O. Hampson & P. Aall (eds.), *Turbulent Peace: The Challenges of Managing International Conflict.* Washington D.C.: United States Institute of Peace Press, pp. 427–443.

Toynbee, Arnold, 1916. 'A Summary of Armenian History up to and Including 1915', in *The Treatment of Armenians in the Ottoman Empire: Documents Presented to Viscount Grey of Falldon, Secretary of State for Foreign Affairs.* London: H.M.S.O.

Tylee, Claire, 1990. *The Great War and Women's Consciousness: Images of Militarism and Womanhood in Women's Writings 1914–64.* Basingstoke: Macmillan.

UCHL, 2005. *Expert Meeting on Private Military Contractors: Status and State Responsibility for their Actions* (ed.). Geneva: University Centre for International Humanitarian Law. 29–30 August.

Ulvros, Eva-Helen, 2005. 'Man kan inte tiga…' Sophie Elkan och fredsfrågan', in Eva Österberg & Marie Lindstedt Cronberg (eds.) *Kvinnor och våld. En mångtydig kulturhistoria.* Lund: Nordic Academic Press, pp. 201–218.

United Nations, 2000. Comprehensive Review of the Whole Question of Peacekeeping Operations in all Their Aspects (A/55/305–S/2000/809). New York: Department of Peacekeeping, United Nations Secretariat.

–, 2005. 'The Impact of Mercenary Activities on the Right of Peoples to Self-Determination', OHCHR Fact Sheet. New York: United Nations Secretariat.

–, 2008. *United Nations Peacekeeping Operations: Principles and Guidelines.* New York: Department of Peacekeeping Operations, United Nations Secretariat.

–, 2008. United Nations Assistance Mission in Afghanistan (UNAMA),

'Overview', available at: http://www.unama-afg.org/about/overview.htm, last accessed 1 December 2008.

United Nations, General Assembly, 1997. Report on the question of the use of mercenaries as a means of violating human rights and impending the exercise of the right of peoples to self-determiniation (A/52/495). New York: United Nations Secretariat, available at http://www.ohchr.org/english/issues/mercenaries/annual.htm

–, 2007. Report on the question of the use of mercenaries as a means of violating human rights and impending the exercise of the right of peoples to self-determiniation (A/62/150). New York: United Nations Secretariat, available at http://www2.ohchr.org/english/issues/mercenaries/index.htm

United Nations Security Council, 2000. Security Council Resolution 1325. 12 April, (SC/RES/1325).

–, 2001. Security Council Resolution 1386, (SC/RES/1386).

United States Institute of Peace, 'Afghan Experience Project, Interview #26', available at: http://www.usip.org/library/oh/sops/afghanistan/gov/26.pdf>, last accessed 5 May 2007.

US State Department, 2008. Daily Press Briefing, with spokesman Sean McCormack, 16 September, available at: http://www.state.gov/r/pa/prs/dpb/2008/sept/109775.htm, accessed 24 September 2008.

–, 2008. Special Briefing 'On-the-Record Briefing With Acting Assistant Secretary of State for Diplomatic Security Gregory B. Starr', April 4 available at: http://www.state.gov/r/pa/prs/ps/2008/apr/102999.htm, accessed 24 September 2008.

Ury, William L., 2000. *The Third Side: Why We Fight and How We Can Stop*. New York: Penguin Books.

Uyangoda, Jayadeva, (ed.), 2005. *Conflict, Conflict Resolution & Peace Building*. Colombo: Colombo University.

–, 2006. 'Sri Lanka: Dimensions of the Crisis', *Polity* 3(4), pp. 3–6.

–, 2007a. *Ethnic Conflict in Sri Lanka: Changing Dynamics*. Washington D.C.: East-West Center.

–, 2007b. 'Politics of Sri Lanka in 2007', *Polity* 4(4), pp. 3–15.

Van der Kloet, Irene, 2006. 'Building Trust in the Mission Area: A Weapon Against Terrorism?', *Small Wars & Insurgencies* 17(4), pp. 421–436.

Vasquez, John & Marie Henehan, 2001. 'Territorial Disputes and the Probability of War, 1816–1992', *Journal of Peace Research* 38(2), pp. 123–38.

Voluntary Principles on Security and Human Rights, available at: http://www.voluntaryprinciples.org.

Washington Post, 2007. 'Blackwater Faulted in Military Reports from Shooting Scene', 5 October, available at: http://www.washintongpost.com

–, 2007. 'Blackwater Chief Defends Firm', 3 October, available at: http://www.washingtonpost.com.

Walker, Clive & David Whyte, 2005. 'Contracting Out War? Private Military Companies, Law and Regulation in the United Kingdom', *International Comparative Law Quarterly* 54, pp. 651–690.

Wall, James A. & John B. Stark, 1996. 'Techniques and Sequences in Mediation Strategies: A Proposed Model for Research', *Negotiation Journal* 12(3), pp. 231–239.

Walters, Barbara F, 2002. *Committing the Peace. The Successful Settlement of Civil Wars*. Princeton/Oxford: Princeton University Press.

Wanigasekera, Edward, Theophilus, 2008. 'The Reality of Oil Dream in Sri Lanka', *Asian Tribune*, 15 September.

Weerasinghe, Mahinda, 2005. 'Kissinger, Nobel Committee, Kissinginian Mutants, or how Norway became a Sanctuary for Terrorists', in *Peace in Sri Lanka: Obstacles and Opportunities*. Nugegoda: World Alliance for Peace in Sri Lanka.

Welsh, Jennifer M., 2004a. 'Introduction', in Jennifer M. Welsh (ed.), *Humanitarian Intervention and International Relations*. Oxford: Oxford University Press.

–, (ed.), 2004b. *Humanitarian Intervention and International Relations*. Oxford: Oxford University Press.

Wilder, Andrew, 2007. 'Cops or Robbers? The Struggle to Reform the Afghan National Police', *AREU Issue Paper Series*, available at: http://www.areu.org.af/index.php?option=com–docman&task=doc–download&gid=523, last accessed 16 December 2008.

Wilson, A.J., 2000. *Sri Lankan Tamil Nationalism: Its Origins And Development in the Nineteenth and Twentieth Centuries*. London: Hurst & Co.

Winks, Robin W. (ed.), 1999. *The Oxford History of the British Empire. Volume V. Historiography*. Oxford & New York: Oxford University Press.

Winter, Jay, Geoffrey Parker & Mary R. Habeck (eds.), 2000. *The Great War and the Twentieth Century*. New Haven & London: Yale University Press.

Woodhouse, Tom, 1999. 'The Gentle Hand of Peace? British Peacekeeping and Conflict Resolution in Complex Political Emergencies', *International Peacekeeping* 6(2), pp. 24–37.

Wriggins, Howard, 1995. 'Sri Lanka: Negotiations in a Secessionist Conflict', in I.W. Zartman (ed.) *Elusive Peace: Negotiating an End to Civil Wars*. Washington D.C.: Brookings.

Yegenouglu, Meyda, 1998. *Colonial Fantasies: Towards a Feminist Reading of Orientalism*. Cambridge: Cambridge University Press.

Zamparelli, Colonel Steven J., 1999. 'Competitive Sourcing and Privatization: Contractors on the Battlefield', *Air Force Journal of Logistics* XXIII, pp. 1–17.

Zarate, Juan Carlos, 1998. 'The Emergence of a New Dog of War: Private

International Security Companies, International Law and the New World Disorder', *Stanford Journal of International Law* 34, pp. 75–162.

Zartman, William I., 1985. *Ripe for Resolution: Conflict and Intervention in Africa.* New York: Oxford University Press.

–, (ed.), 1995. *Elusive Peace: Negotiating an End to Civil War.* Washington D.C.: Brookings Institute.

–, 2000. 'Ripeness: The Hurting Stalemate and Beyond', in P.C. Stern & Daniel Druckman (eds.) *International Conflict Resolution After the Cold War.* Washington, D.C.: National Academy Press.

–, & Guy Olivier Faure (eds.), 2005. *Escalation and Negotiation in International Conflicts.* Cambridge: Cambridge University Press.

Index